*Before I felt grey, on the edges
and nobody noticed me.
And now – it's like a painting.
I'm in the middle and painted
in bright colours.*

*(James Howlet, aged 9.
Monteclefe Junior School, Somerton;
by kind permission of Nadia Rice,
School-based Special Educational Needs Teacher)*

Quality Circle Time in the Primary Classroom

Your essential guide to enhancing self-esteem, self-discipline and positive relationships

Jenny Mosley

Quality Circle Time in the Primary Classroom
LD 1034
ISBN 1 85503 229 5
© Jenny Mosley
Photographs George Solomonides
All rights reserved
First published 1996
Reprinted 1996, 1997

LDA, Duke Street, Wisbech, Cambs, PE13 2AE

Thanks to Marlborough First and Middle School, Harrow,
for their kind co-operation with the photography.

Contents

Reviews and Responses to Jenny Mosley's Turn Your School Round

Jenny Mosley's book presents a very persuasive rationale for adopting Circle-Time as an integral part of the school's curriculum ... Turn Your School Round is an ambitious book ... The methods proposed by Jenny Mosley are informed by the recognition that self-esteem is central to promoting appropriate behaviour in adults and children ... I feel that this book is an invaluable resource for schools and can be recommended to anyone who works with children.

Rory Gordon
Special Children April 1994

I found the book useful and will recommend it to schools ... It is reasonably priced and offers a well-rounded model on which to embark on a whole-school approach, in this important and increasingly topical area of policy development.

Fran Hill
Support for Learning Vol 9 No 3 (1994)

The presentation of ideas and examples is beautifully clear ... There is a wealth of examples of playground games and other ideas aimed at preventing problems ...

Self-Esteem Network Newsletter
Autumn 1994 Issue 6

The publication of this book is timely as contact with primary schools indicates strongly that many are currently tackling the effective curriculum, involving non-teaching staff in related inservice work and are returning to the focus on parental involvement, it builds on current school review and planning requirements and takes schools towards the development of a whole school behaviour policy.

Anne Edwards, Education Section Review
British Psychological Society

Arguably, Jenny Mosley has taken what industry and business calls Total Quality Management and given it a primary school "feel".

The best British firms have been learning for some time now that listening to the workforce and making them feel part of the operation makes for more efficiency than does any amount of financial inducement or end-of-process inspection.

Gerald Haigh
Times Educational Supplement 1994

Turn Your School Round makes available to schools committed to mutual understanding and co-operation, ways of valuing and using communication as an important tool in the development of self-esteem and learning capacities. It is strongly recommended.

Heather Geddes and Gill Morton
Journal for Forum of the Advancement of Educational Therapy

One of the many strong points in the book is the section that helps you identify how unmet human needs lead to low self-esteem and negative ways of relating to people and describes stages by which self-esteem and self-realisation is actualised. I was also particularly impressed with the guidelines for making good relationships with children ...

Primary Teaching Studies Journal Spring 1993

I'm recommending Turn Your School Round as a must for every school. There are so many good ideas and it's such a delight to read.

Primary Headteacher

I found Turn Your School Round encouraging, reassuring and uplifting to read. Most of all I found it pleasurable.

Health Promotion Specialist
Schools/Young People

The book is great, useful, full of helpful practical ideas, thought provoking, creative, easy to follow, well presented, teacher friendly but above all (for me) of real benefit to schools and children ... it's all about central issues for schools.

Senior Educational Psychologist

It has been very encouraging to hear, from many witnesses, of the success of her work in improving good schools and "turning round" those in difficulty, as it endorses some of the Committee's most important findings. It therefore gives me great pleasure to commend her book to other teachers who may profit from her experience and advice.

Lord Elton – Chairman of HMSO Report
'Discipline in Schools'

Acknowledgements – A personal chapter

I have decided to really enjoy writing this section even though I'm not sure I'll be allowed to get it into the book!

I am always encouraging adults and children in schools to write positive diaries and to celebrate all their achievements and positive events. One lovely school I have worked with now has its own 'Happy Book' – anybody in school or any visitor who says something positive about any aspect of the school is immediately asked to write it down in their special book. The headteacher also puts in any 'thank you' letters. Whenever they are feeling a little down somebody can be found flicking through the Happy Book. The smallest thing is recorded, from a child smiling who normally finds it difficult to greet the day warmly to a parent's positive comment. It is therefore obvious that the spirit of this book demands that I too celebrate the wonderful support I receive. No doubt as a start to an academic book this section is hopelessly colloquial, self-indulgent and 'over-the-top' and will deter loads of potential customers ... Still, I'd urge you all to attempt a similar task in order to celebrate all the good people who have quietly (or loudly) helped you over the years, and then tuck this 'jewel' away for perusal during the bleak moments.

By writing down the names of all the people who have been supportive and helpful I will have a treasure box to sift through when I have low days or when the going seems tough. My only concern is that once I try to mention and record significant people in my life, there is a huge danger that, being rushed and frail of memory, I am bound to leave important people out. Please forgive me in advance. I promise I will remedy it in the future!

Professional support

Firstly, I would like to thank Jo Browning Wroe, my lovely, patient editor, who is now a good friend. We have difficult times as well as good ones. We seem to survive by trying to be flexible and understand each other's busy lives. Jo has now edited three of my books and I appreciate her cool vision and warm enthusiasm. She set out to understand my packed life and strongly held philosophies and has accompanied me with empathy along the way.

Simon Lyne, LDA's managing director, is also a source of strength. He has given me time and help beyond the call of publishing duty and greets my hare-brained schemes with an equal amount of energy and interest.

Marion Bennathan, Lord Elton, David Fontana and Peter Robinson, all key people in education and fantastic pioneers in their own right, have helped me along the way. In the early days especially their words of support and interest in my initiatives were a great source of energy for me.

Since those early days my freelance educational consultancy work across the UK has flourished and I am now extremely fortunate that there are key LEA personnel who manage to keep bringing me back to their area, year after year, to work in a very productive and exciting way with some of their schools. Special thanks must go to the following:

> David Bottomley and Elaine Doxey in Barnsley
> Jan Chappell and Sally Fox in Hertfordshire
> Bridgeen O'Neill, Mary Blease, Jim Tiernan, Denise Burke and
>   Ginny Hamilton from Belfast
> Sandy Chapman from Cornwall
> Nick Peacey from London University, who also contributed to
>   Part Five
> My four musketeers from Scotland – Marjory Marshall,
>   Lina Waghorn, Rosanna Wood and Sharon Johnston
> Avril Topping and Carol Howard from Cheshire
> Ronnie Sullivan, Mary Smith and Simon Burke from Wiltshire
> Breda O'Reilly Hogan and Jim Connolly from Dublin
> Liz Robson from Camden, who also contributed important
>   links between Circle Time and the National Curriculum
>   (see Part Five).

Apart from these people being visionary and dedicated, two important qualities in education, when we meet we have some great laughs. In their part of the country there is always warmth and humour.

Practical support

I could not cope without the tolerant understanding and practical support of my wonderful network of secretarial assistants, Helen Gowen, Kay Hardwick, Maureen Harvey and Heather Timbrell. They are great women who manage to cope under the unusual circumstances they work in – which can involve my own three children leaping and shrieking around, the dog yapping madly most of the day and a hamster that thinks it is Houdini. Despite all this they keep calm and, what is more, keep coming back – thank God!

Helen Sonnet is one of the above team of secretaries and she has been particularly creative, patient and helpful with me over this book. We have slaved together over ideas and she has kept my flagging enthusiasm going when I felt I would rather have a good sleep. She is an amazing woman in her own right, bringing up her four girls to be creative and kind-hearted people.

Kim McClurg is wonderful in the way she steps in and helps me with the house or the children when I'm going up the wall.

Visionary support

Titus Alexander is a noble spearhead for the Self Esteem Network which gathers all like-minded people under a big strong umbrella to try to unite people and initiate change in a more global way. Murray White must be thanked for his role in creating two wonderful self-esteem conferences which gave me personally a real boost of enthusiasm. Gerda Hanko has inspired me with her own book and her unfailing words of kindness and support whenever we have met. Dr Mary Grant, Dr Nona Dawson and Fil Came (WEST) give me great support by sharing my vision regarding the role of Circle Time in education. They are brilliant researchers and it is a comfort to be involved with them as a team.

Lastly, I would like to thank the late Chris Fletcher from Salterns School. As a teacher at a school for children with severe learning difficulties she had an extraordinary vision of the quality of life that should be shared by the whole school community. She used to refer to her staff as her 'rainbow', meaning that all the adults' different qualities enveloped the school in a warm and beautiful strength. I often, now, think of different teams as 'rainbows'.

Student support

Although it is incredibly hard work combining my teaching at Bristol University with my freelance work, I do get great joy from my students and I have had some wonderful students in the last two years who keep me in touch through the special light that they take with them to the areas that they work in. In particular I would like to thank Caroline Mann and Viv Stevens who – along with their very supportive, understanding husbands, Michael and Simon – have endeavoured to help me to become more businesslike and more capable of moving forward in an organised and dynamic way. They are all successful, busy people and yet they always find the time to write notes and create meetings to help further the Circle-Time 'cause'.

Family and friends

Where do I start thanking family and friends? My mother, Veronica Orr, is an amazing woman. She also has brought up three children on her own and yet always created fun time and always gave us total listening support when we needed it. My sister, Edwina Orr, having left home at 15 and school at 16, has forged an incredible path through life. Apart from being an artist she is also a creative genius (well, I think so) as she has, with her partner David, just invented holographic 3-dimensional television; I find her inspiring.

My friends put up with an awful lot. I am always busy or on the move and yet they know I need and love to celebrate the good times, especially with wild dancing to loud music or long wine-soaked chats. So lots of thanks must go to my very close pals, Mary Martin, Freda Keys, Sarah Bates, Sarah Bishop, Angie Russ, Jo Dyer, Rob and Fatima, Dee Russell, Alice Naish, Jean Chancellor, Wendy Joslin, Tom Oliva, Cheryl Drower, Lucilia Valente and Pam Maxwell.

Special thanks to Elizabeth Guettier from France who once listened to a radio programme that mentioned *Turn Your School Round* and then dedicated lots of her own, and her young friends', time to translating it into French in the hope that one day it may contribute to the French educational system!

Eileen Gillibrand is a wonderful friend and colleague. She and I set up a small company specifically to support women and have written books and made videos together whilst cooking suppers, signing children's notes and clutching mugs of coffee and shrieking with laughter.

My children and I!

Now, with all the support I have mentioned above, you would think that life would be very easy. In fact because of all the travelling and the initiating and sustaining of new projects in lots of different areas, I am often exhausted and frazzled so it is no good my writing a glowing tribute to my children as if I were some sort of brilliant mother. I do think David, Meg and Sally are wonderful, but in their feisty adolescence, I can fail to practise what I preach and I am sometimes a pain to live with (so are they!).

So, it is not all 'self-esteem and Circle Time' in our house. Mind you, there are occasions when they are all roaring and wailing and we do introduce the Circle-Time speaking object. The only problem is that they rugby tackle each other to get the object off that person so that they can carry on monopolising the debate. I should have started it all much earlier. I think it is incredibly hard being a good enough parent and I have such admiration for all the parents who juggle their careers and children with sensitivity and care. Still, despite all the frayed tempers and the tiredness we have some great times, especially during the summer music festivals where we all dance and on firelit winter evenings when we watch American soaps and munch chocolate.

To all schools

And now, obviously, I must say 'thank you' to the thousands of schools who practise this approach and continue to invite me in and to be open to change. I have a huge respect for teachers and an enduring appreciation for children's honesty and innate wisdom. Thank you, especially, to all the individual teachers and schools who have contributed to this book. They may not see their name mentioned but hopefully they'll recognise their words.

I am privileged to be in this circle work as I do get great joy from it.

Preface

Circle Time has recently become a 'buzz' term in education, and like any new trend it is vulnerable to misuse and abuse. I have heard it applied equally to a superficial newsround where children shouted out one-word responses and to a worryingly intense discussion amongst pupils about an absent peer; in both cases the teachers had failed to adhere to the basic Circle-Time groundrules or structures I advocate, and to understand fully its true potential as a forum for individual and organisational change.

My own involvement with Circle Time

Over twenty years ago, whilst teaching in an inner-city school, I was introduced to a form of circular discussion meeting initiated by an inspiring headteacher. Through my extra evening and holiday teaching experiences of initiating drama and active groupwork sessions from within the circle forum in youth clubs, play-centres and holiday schemes, I explored many experiential strategies with various poignant shades of failure and success.

Throughout my subsequent long and varied career in primary, secondary and special education and my parallel training and therapeutic work with adults and children, I continued to develop my own Circle-Time methods as a means of promoting self-esteem, self-discipline and responsibility towards others. I eventually developed a whole-school Circle-Time management model that I felt could encompass many of the educational and personal needs of adults and children.

For the past eight years, as a freelance educational consultant, I have worked across the United Kingdom in hundreds of schools and run courses for thousands of individual teachers as well as for learning and behavioural support teams, educational psychologists, PSE, health and primary advisers, hospital and special needs teachers and whole-school communities including children, parents and support staff wanting to promote this model.

In 1987 a year-long project I ran for Wiltshire LEA, which involved me in leading a group of teachers researching and trialling a range of Circle-Time and self-esteem methods in their own classes, came to fruition with the publication of *All Round Success* (Mosley, 1989); and in 1993 LDA published my *Turn Your School Round* (Mosley, 1993), which gives structured help to those responsible for contributing to primary school development. Lord Elton wrote the foreword, commenting that the book endorsed some of his committee's most important findings, as reported in the *Elton Report* (Elton, 1989). The response to this book was one of overwhelming interest and support. Many schools are now acting on its recommendations and through the forum of timetabled Circle-Time meetings have received excellent OFSTED reports in the area of personal, social, cultural, spiritual and moral education.

However, the rapid groundswell of interest in Circle Time has brought its own drawbacks. Some teachers, immersed in the sudden flurry of new books and materials relating to Circle Time, without access to an understanding of the whole model, have found themselves struggling to find a way forward. These developments have left the original Circle-Time model, as I initially structured it, open to dilution and pollution. I am definitely not saying that there aren't many excellent Circle-Time influences other than my own (see Resources section). Nevertheless, based on my many years of practical Circle-Time experiences, I advocate a specific whole-school model that ties in all the other school systems which influence behaviour and relationships. For me, its strength lies precisely in the fact that Circle-Time meetings act as the forum through which to deliver these strategies, so that the model itself is circular (see A Circular Model, page 31).

In the light of these developments, I decided it was important to write another handbook to support the teacher whose whole school community is attempting the approach; and also the teacher who as an individual wishes to take the circle model into her classroom but isn't, as yet, within a team who are all working in the same way. In order to consult some teachers currently using my model, I sent out a questionnaire to a range of schools I had worked in during the previous five years. I asked them to complete the questionnaire as honestly as possible in order that I could discover how their Circle Times were progressing, what problems they had encountered and what further support they would like. The returned questionnaires were enormously positive about the benefits of timetabled Circle Time, but many teachers were desperate for more ideas for activities and games, for ways of developing these and suggestions for how to overcome specific problems. I have, therefore, created a large section of further Circle-Time ideas presented in theories and I have distilled the most common classroom dilemmas into a separate chapter, 'Teachers Talk Back'.

Definitions of 'quality' invariably include the concepts of 'essential characteristics' or 'degree of excellence'. I hope, in this book, to outline what I believe to be the key features of Circle Time, which, if adhered to, will contribute to a programme of 'excellence'.

A whole-school approach based on creating bridges between circles

Despite the fact that I am aiming this book towards the classroom teacher, I must state from the outset that the ideal school for me is one in which every child and adult belongs to a programme of timetabled Circle-Time meetings. Teachers need at least one staff meeting per half-term where they don't have to discuss 'business' or National Curriculum issues, but can instead focus on their feelings. They need to talk through various dilemmas, to take time to understand certain difficult children, to ask for help with discipline or curriculum concerns without being judged, or to discuss problems with parents and then ask for support in structuring action plans that will help them move forward. Lunchtime supervisors, ancillary helpers, secretaries and caretakers also need to have their own circle meetings (ideally all adults should share some circle meetings together, but lack of time in school makes this hugely impractical). Consequently some schools negotiate a programme of circle meetings which, even if they are only two half-hour sessions each half-term, can be very effective.

As staff and children become involved in their separate circle meetings, it's vital they link together by means of 'bridges'. The concept is that the pivotal management circle should consist of the teaching staff, and the news, ideas and concerns from the other circles all need to reach them if they are to make informed management decisions based on a democratic consultation of all the members of the organisation. Therefore, a person must be selected from every circle to create a 'bridge' to the inner management circle by simply taking from their circle meeting, with the agreement of the other circle members, all the points of change or information that need to be noted to the pivotal circle. At some stage they have to return across the bridge with some feedback or response to their concerns or ideas.

A real quality circle

Again, in an ideal world, I would love to see this group of representatives all meeting together at least once a term. A quality circle, in my view, would consist of two teachers representing school management, two children from every class, two parents, two learning support assistants, two playground supervisors and two representatives of ancillary staff. I recognise this vision to be, as yet, merely a hope, but I invite all readers to share and promote this vision with me. The reality is, however, that time is a precious and shrinking resource in schools and that it's good enough that the information, either verbal or written, reaches the staff circle whenever the appointed person can dash across that rickety fragile bridge.

Many classroom teachers, reading the above, are going to give exasperated, weary sighs, muttering that there's no chance of this notion of 'quality' ever entering their exhausted and overstretched school. I totally understand this view, but ask you at least to bear with the next section of this preface, so you can share a wider understanding with me. I promise you, the book is about what you, as an individual, can do to achieve excellence within your own classroom.

The wider vision: a team approach

My daily experience of working with different schools means that I have a deep empathy with teachers regarding the trials they face. Basically, I see most teachers as warm-hearted, good people weighed down by a range of burgeoning demands. Consequently, some are losing sight of the original vision that inspired them to enter teaching in the first place, a vision that was once infused with their own joy in learning, deep regard for all children and a belief that they could effect positive changes. Instead I see some schools where teachers are wearily trudging up a huge mountain and are so bowed down by pressures and worries that they are unable to glimpse the vision they are supposed to be trying to reach. Snowstorms of paper every now and then whistle around and shroud them from each other. Boulders in the shape of large ring-binder files whizz past their heads, arriving somewhere from the top of the mountain, whilst every now and then parents and governors leap out from bushes brandishing sheaves of paper and claiming certain rights. If the individuals in this school attempt to climb the mountain on their own, they are likely to disappear into swamps or silently fall off cliff edges without anyone noticing. The only way to go up is by forming a team and linking arms; the strength gained from the linking together means that the team can carry one or two members who are on their knees because of physical exhaustion or maybe problems at home.

As an individual you are happy to help out as you are safe in the knowledge that, should you need it, the team will carry you at some other time in the term. The team approach demands that no-one can remain on her knees for the whole term but also allows individuals to pace themselves. You don't have to be bright, enthusiastic and strong every day; you can take it in turns along with others. In other words, the team does not leave it up to certain members to take the weight; everyone contributes as much as she possibly can.

No perks in education

There is a great irony about the mountain metaphor. Should you be in industry and your team be exhausted or suffering from low morale, your company may well be gathered up and taken to a real mountain where you and your team would scale real hills, traverse real swamps, abseil down real cliffs and when pleasurably physically tired would wander down to a lovely valley at the bottom of the mountain where, lo and behold, there was a luxurious hotel where you would all be treated to wonderful food and drink and later sit in a circle to play fun games together. What do they call this day out? TEAM BUILDING! I almost feel guilty going around schools with the rallying cry, 'You should all become part of a supportive and respectful team,' when I know that, yet again, teachers are being asked to achieve another goal without being given any of the perks or luxuries given elsewhere. But unfortunately there's no avoiding the issue; the only way forward is for all the adults in the school to look into their hearts and ask themselves how good a team member they are: 'How much do I give, how much do I take from the team?'

We all affect each other: collective responsibility

When I enter each new school I see all the teaching and support staff as an upright circle of dominoes. If any of those dominoes is in a bad mood or a negative state of mind, it has the power to knock down all the others. In other words, you can meet someone's mood without actually meeting him or her. Children are lightning conductors of adults' moods – they scan our faces, listen intently to our tone of voice and within minutes can be profoundly affected. If a teacher is in a negative mood, she can wind up her children into such a state that they burst into the playground as her exact replicas, intent on irritating all the other children. The children whose lunchtimes have been ruined then rush back after lunch to their own classes, quarrelsome and distracted – hence their waiting teacher meets the first teacher's early morning mood! It is vital that staff understand this concept and take time to foster collective responsibility towards each other, the first step for which must be setting up quality circle meetings for all the adults. The vision of enhancing staff morale and self-esteem through a Circle Time policy is not one you can aspire to if the senior management doesn't share it. Nevertheless, you can take on the concept of personal responsibility by acknowledging that one of your most important priorities, essential for your colleagues and children, is to be as positive, enthusiastic and energetic a person as possible given the circumstances!

Language relating to gender

Note that in general a teacher is referred to as 'she'. An individual child is referred to as 'he' or as 'she'; the usage alternates between chapters.

References

Elton, Lord (1989) *Discipline in Schools*, Report of Committee of Enquiry Chaired by Lord Elton, London: HMSO.

Mosley, J. (1989) *All Round Success*, Wiltshire County Council (available from Advisory Education Services, County Hall, Trowbridge, Wiltshire BA14 8JB).

Mosley, J. (1993) *Turn Your School Round*, Cambridge: LDA.

PART 1

Working on Yourself

How to establish positive relationships in your class

Relationships are built when individuals feel valued and respected. Being listened to helps each child feel unique and worthwhile. It is, therefore, important to reassure children that they can, if they really need to, become the legitimate focus of your attention through the various listening systems that you set up for them. Yet often we look so harassed and busy that children are put off trying to speak to us. The ensuing sense of frustration or even isolation can later drive them to demand the much needed attention by anti-social means such as sulking, defying or arguing. After all, negative attention is better than none.

Consequently, we need to help each child feel that access to our attention is there if he needs it. Consider first whether your attitude towards each child would really encourage him to approach you. Look through the following pointers and reflect on whether you offer each child a positive, valuing relationship.

- Do I genuinely like all the children in my class?
- Do I really care about each child in my class?
- Can I find something good in each child?
- Do I speak respectfully to each child?
- Am I able to avoid confrontation?
- Am I able to forgive every child?
- Do I regularly acknowledge the positive attributes of each child?
- Do I expect certain children to misbehave?
- Do I assume certain children are guilty before establishing the facts?

- Am I able to apologise to any child if I have reacted unjustly?
- Is my body language consistent with the words I use to each child?
- Do I organise the curriculum so that it's possible for every child to achieve daily moments of success, which I then take time to notice?

Remember that for a few children you offer the only unconditional warmth and respect they experience in their lives and you may be the only contributor to their fragile sense of self-worth.

Perhaps one of the most important aspects that we all need to remember is that we, the teachers, are the inspiring role models for our children. It is unfair to ask or expect children to be calm, polite, sensitive and responsible if our own behaviour towards them or our colleagues does not reflect these values. Some teachers in difficult situations seem to find themselves fighting a never-ending battle to create a well-disciplined climate. Ironically, this battle can involve them in shouting, sarcasm, temper flare-ups or other negative responses, all of which confirm some children's beliefs that this is how people relate to one another.

Don't be demoralised into thinking that some teachers are naturally 'good' at discipline whilst you just don't seem to have 'the knack'. Classroom skills for promoting positive behaviour and good relationships can be learnt and strategies can be adopted which will enhance your ability to achieve more positive behaviour within the classroom. These will be dealt with more fully in later sections. Initially, what we need to do is assess our own behaviour towards the children. The following advice may seem very obvious, but when we are stressed we sometimes can lose sight of our contribution to negative perception and need to spend a few minutes being very honest with ourselves.

Examining ourselves

It is vital, though often difficult, to treat each child as an individual and to avoid any preconceived, often unconscious, judgements based on past experiences, catchment areas or family reputations. Every child has the right to be judged on his own unique strengths. Besides this, if you expect a child to behave badly because, for example, he comes from a known family of 'offenders', your expectations and your verbal and non-verbal responses towards that child will be different from those that you use with the other children. He then feels alienated and distanced from you and 'plays up' even more. You could, therefore, be trapping that child into a self-fulfilling negative cycle of unacceptable behaviour.

We need to consider first the language that we use with all or some of the children. Is it non-threatening or do the tone and words convey threat? Children react either defensively or aggressively to threatening language, either direct or suggested. It might be useful to set aside one day and make a mental or written note of the tone and language that you have used. If you are very open and brave ask a colleague to come in and watch the way you respond to the children and give you some feedback afterwards. If you think that much of what you say is negative then, if necessary, write out and practise some alternative, positive dialogues. Set aside a few minutes each day to engage in a genuinely positive conversation with a child that you find it difficult to relate to. Don't be discouraged into thinking that you can't change; you can. You are as capable of effecting change in yourself as you are of helping others to change.

Examining our language

Try to develop the ability to use objective language when describing specific unacceptable behaviour, so that, for example, 'Jack was very naughty this morning' becomes 'Jack left his seat six times before lunchtime.'

It is far easier for a child to concentrate on not leaving his seat or not talking out of turn than to respond to a generalised instruction to 'be good' or 'behave well'. Don't forget, when we ask a child to 'behave well', we are imposing on him our image of an ideal child and there may be too big a mismatch between this ideal self and his actual self for him to cope with. Children can feel the wide gap between your expectations of how they should be and how they actually are, and the distance can be overwhelming for them. If you swamp the children with unrealistic demands they cannot move forward; the way to help them is to find a tiny, achievable, tickable target (see page 53). Also, it is important that the teacher's disapproval is focused on the act and not on the personality or character of the child; it is then unacceptable behaviour you reject, not the whole child. Therefore the teacher might say, 'I feel angry with you when you leave your seat during work time,' rather than 'You make me angry'; or, 'I cannot concentrate if you talk when I am speaking to you,' instead of 'You are a very rude little boy.'

The power of praise

Above all, it is important that the teacher praises good behaviour to reinforce what is expected of children. Many teachers spend a disproportionate amount of time emphasising what the children should not do, rather than focusing on desired behaviours. Take time to recognise and praise these moments, however few, when all the children are working well. Look out for and congratulate individual children who are upholding the class's Golden Rules. It is too easy to neglect making positive comments in the effort to maintain classroom discipline. Make sure also that you constantly use an incentive system. Sometimes we become so exhausted and bad-tempered that we stop using incentives; this, in turn, forces the children to gain negative attention from you and, before long, you are all once again sliding down a slippery slope of negativity. If, for example, the teacher finds that the level of noise within the classroom is frequently louder than she is happy with, it is better for her to devise a positive system with the children to reduce the noise level, than constantly to shout for silence. The system could be 'hands up' for silence, whereby the teacher raises a hand and the children follow suit, raising their hands and becoming silent. The teacher then puts her hand down before she starts to speak again. If a system like this is used the teacher should try to ensure that she doesn't request silence just for negative reasons, for example, to say how cross she is because they are working too noisily. Every now and then she needs to raise her hand to say, 'I just want to congratulate you all on your level of concentration.'

Once you have taken responsibility for examining your own role in promoting positive relationships and a valuing ethos in the classroom, it becomes possible to establish systems in the class that can support and reinforce the moral values that underlie your aim to create good relationships and respect for self and for others.

We are human, too

We, the teachers, must also accept that it is all right for us to make mistakes, get things wrong and apologise when we are at fault. It will not diminish our authority to admit to human flaws; it can only enhance it. It also encourages children to realise that it is all right to make mistakes as long as you try to acknowledge them and to say sorry, should you have hurt anyone else.

I knew a lovely teacher who, in a Circle-Time session, decided that it was her turn during Open Forum to ask for help with her behaviour. She simply said, 'I need help because I sometimes feel irritable and niggly in the afternoon and I'd like to change.' The first 'helper' raised her hand and suggested, 'Would it help if you let us know when this horrible feeling was coming over you?' A second helper then put up his hand and said, 'Miss, would it help if you put on a special hat to let us know when you were getting cross?' Calm, peaceful afternoons now reign in that class. Whenever the teacher feels her blood-pressure rising, she reaches for her big straw hat, which signifies to the children that they should keep quiet. The very sight of them exaggeratedly whispering and tip-toeing around the classroom brings a smile to her face and soon, with a flourish, she can take off the hat and the bad mood and hang them back up on the peg. I know life isn't always this simple, but admitting you're human and asking for help sometimes from the children really can help foster the team spirit.

Starting with yourself

We can genuinely find many things to blame when we become tired, bad-tempered or worried. Consider just a few of the following factors, which individual teachers often face on a daily basis:

- growing administrative pressures,
- pressure of pupil performance,
- children with severe emotional and behavioural problems,
- lack of colleague or parental support,
- inadequate resources,
- demands from home/family,
- lack of respect from society.

It is small wonder that some hard-pressed teachers find themselves resorting to defensive actions in an effort to survive the rigors of the classroom. The more we become caught up in negative interactions, the more our self-esteem is lowered.

Research (Burns, 1982) shows that teachers with low self-esteem find it very difficult to raise the self-esteem of their pupils. Teachers with high self-esteem are far more able to enhance the self-esteem of others. It is vital, if we want to do the best for the children we teach, that we find ways of becoming more positive, energetic, courageous and consistent.

Initially, it is important to check your own self-esteem in order to assess the sort of support, help or action plan you may need to carry out. Look through the following list of pointers; if you find you're saying 'yes' to too many, then maybe you really need to spend time working on yourself. If you find these pointers don't really apply to you, then you still deserve to spend more time on yourself in order to maintain your positive outlook and give yourself even more energy.

Pointers To Help You Assess Your Self-esteem

1 Do you often lose your temper with the children?
2 Do you worry about asking colleagues for help?
3 Are you envious of colleagues?
4 Do you worry about work when you're at home?
5 Do you continually complain about situations/events at work?
6 Do you have personality clashes with certain children/colleagues?

7 Do you feel that your efforts to make improvements are ineffective?
8 Do you need to shout to gain pupils' attention?
9 Do you often give punishments for poor behaviour?
10 Are you nervous of trying out new ideas with your pupils?
11 Do you expect problems from children with certain backgrounds/families?
12 Are you often absent through illness?
13 Do you often struggle on with headaches or other stress conditions?
14 Do you become very defensive if criticised?
15 Do you tend to reject praise by making a joke of it?
16 Do you find it hard to praise children or colleagues?

The following diagrams illustrate the effects of different kinds of self-esteem.

POOR SELF-ESTEEM MEANS

A negative view of yourself with no real awareness of your personal strengths and needs. Low self-worth creates feelings of worthlessness and an inability to be objective about negative incidents; everything feels as if it's your fault or life is conspiring to get you down. You begin to take everything personally.

LEADS TO

LEADS TO

Low self-confidence. You have difficulty in being clear and direct when expressing your needs and ideas. Lack of confidence leads to fear of failure, an unwillingness to take on fresh challenges and an inability to cope when things go wrong.

Poor Self-esteem

Lower self-confidence. Your relationship skills become weaker. You may become passive or aggressive or manipulative. You begin to feel that life is a constant battle in which you are on the losing side. You become prickly or withdrawn towards people.

LEADS TO

LEADS TO

Lower self-esteem. You perceive that others do not respect you or consider your feelings or requests, which further weakens your self-image and confirms your opinion that you can't achieve success or personal/ professional fulfilment.

GOOD SELF-ESTEEM MEANS

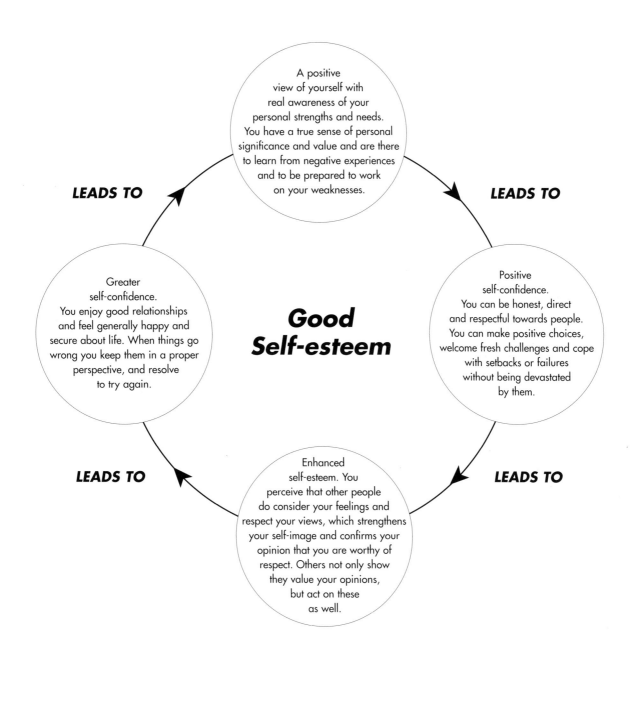

A positive view of yourself with real awareness of your personal strengths and needs. You have a true sense of personal significance and value and are there to learn from negative experiences and to be prepared to work on your weaknesses.

LEADS TO

Positive self-confidence. You can be honest, direct and respectful towards people. You can make positive choices, welcome fresh challenges and cope with setbacks or failures without being devastated by them.

LEADS TO

Good Self-esteem

Enhanced self-esteem. You perceive that other people do consider your feelings and respect your views, which strengthens your self-image and confirms your opinion that you are worthy of respect. Others not only show they value your opinions, but act on these as well.

LEADS TO

Greater self-confidence. You enjoy good relationships and feel generally happy and secure about life. When things go wrong you keep them in a proper perspective, and resolve to try again.

LEADS TO

Work on your own self-esteem

It is vital that we take responsibility for learning how to value our own qualities and strengths. There are times when we don't get the positive acknowledgement or feedback we deserve. When this happens we need to spend time focusing on our positive attributes. Many of us give ourselves a bad time by constantly putting ourselves down and focusing on the negative. We must make a resolution to give equal time (more, if possible) to tease out and focus on all the positive things we are achieving.

The list on the next page will help you make a start in the right direction. Write down any achievement you have made alongside the relevant headings. If you find it difficult to think positively about yourself, be daring and ask a colleague, friend or partner to help you with it.

Making a note of your successes and achievements may help you to be aware of and appreciate the qualities that you possess and give you the self-respect that you deserve. Try in the future, when you are feeling low, to note down any recent positive events to balance your perspective and encourage a more positive outlook. If things are getting you down, try and record all positive happenings in a special 'Happy Book'. It is well known that stress clinics always ask their clients to take time to do this. Why don't you try it, before you become too stressed?

A precious resource

If you can view yourself as a precious resource for children and other adults, then you will understand that you can't go on giving out to others; you'll get burnt out. Like any resource, you need replenishing from time to time. Energy is one of the most important resources you have and in order to sustain the energy that you require to continue to act as a resource for others you must learn how to revitalise yourself by visiting outside 'wells'. Also, there will be times in your life when you need to learn to say 'No!' to others in order to safeguard your own energy. This does not make you a selfish person; it merely makes you someone who is capable of being direct, honest and trustworthy. If you look after your own needs first, you will have more to offer others when they suddenly spring demands on you. The diagram on page 24 will give you an idea of which 'wells' you can visit to replenish your energy.

Write down any achievement you have made alongside the relevant headings.

Any social/school event you have organised.	
Anyone you have helped recently.	
Any way in which you have enhanced your home/school surroundings.	
Any relationship skill you possess.	
Any exercise/sport you are involved in.	
Any book/film you have recently read/seen.	
Any hobby you pursue.	
Any time you have motivated others.	
Any piece of work you did well.	
Any skill that has brought you success.	
Any time you led a new initiative.	
Any skill/knowledge you have recently acquired.	
Any time you contributed to policy-making.	
Any time you successfully coped with a dilemma.	
Any time you received praise from superiors at work.	
Any way you have helped in the social community.	
Any difficult letter/phone call that you handled well.	
Any new challenge you have taken on.	
Any recent relationship success.	
Any other events which have enhanced your life.	

VISITING THE WELLS

Cognitive Well
Reading books.
Watching plays/films.
Debating ideas. Submitting ideas
to others. Planning/structuring
ideas and thinking
things through.

Spiritual Well
This is about renewing your
sense of wonderment and awe.
You may get this from your
religious beliefs, from
meditation or taking time truly
to enter the moments of
contemplating the
beauty of nature.

GIVES
YOU
ENERGY

Emotional Well
Time for fun and enjoying
unconditional time with others.
Friendships, stable loving
relationships with partner/family.
Opportunities to express feelings.
Opportunities to talk through
dilemmas in a supportive
relationship.

Physical Well
It is very difficult to enjoy
mental health if you are
physically tense and heavy
with lethargy. To dissolve knot of
tension, exercise weekly,
learn relaxation techniques,
go for massage, eat
and sleep well.

Creative Well
Enjoy hobbies.
Appreciate art.
Write/draw/sing/tap dance etc.

Personal care plan – based on the Wells Model

It is a good idea to work out a weekly personal care plan to try to ensure that your needs are met. It is all too easy to get so caught up in the pressures of work and home that you neglect your own needs and live life constantly on the edge of exhaustion. Your weekly care plan must make sufficient provision for you to visit the wells, replenish your energy levels, and enjoy yourself. Laughing and having fun is the greatest tonic there is, but adults sometimes lose the ability to do this on a regular basis and suffer greatly through not doing so.

When I advocate personal care plans on my courses, I often meet resistance – particularly from women who say, 'I can't do that, I feel guilty, my family needs me more.' The fact is that you are not an endless resource for others; you must replenish those energy levels and to do this you need to sit down with your partner/family so that you can explain or negotiate certain times of the week which are yours. With tenacity and planning it is possible to encourage others to support you. I was once working with a very stressed teacher, a single parent of young children, who recognised that she was becoming 'burnt out' and agreed to work out a system with her children. It was too difficult to organise child care, so she and the children made a 'DO NOT DISTURB – I'M HAVING A SPECIAL TIME' sign for her. When she put it up the children would allow her five minutes to have a cup of tea or read a book without interruption. After a few months she reported back that although it had been difficult at first, it gradually became easier; in fact, the children had asked to borrow the sign occasionally and part of their 'game' was that she shouldn't disturb them. Over a few weeks, prior to seeing me for the second time, she had been exceptionally busy and was gently reminded of this fact when a small hand went into hers and one of her children said, 'Mum, why haven't you been having your Special Time?'

Survival techniques

In addition to a weekly personal care plan there are other ideas and techniques which can help you to survive the day-to-day pressure of work.

The box that pulsates guilt (or managing time more effectively!)
The most important survival technique is to organise your time efficiently. Decide how much time you will allocate to extra-curricular school-related work and stick to it. Prioritise what needs to be done, so that you deal with important and urgent items first, and be strict with yourself about leaving tasks which are not vital for another day. Do not slip into the trap of adopting a box that pulsates guilt. Most of us effectively carry around a big box or folder full of things to do which we lug from classroom to sitting room and back again. It is so daunting a burden that we can't

face tackling it. It merely rests in the corner of our vision distracting us from getting any real pleasure from our leisure time as every time we catch sight of it we feel guilty. The trick is to prioritise. Only tackle what is undeniably necessary, those which failure to tackle would be observable to all. Many things in the box are only good intentions; they are not strictly needed. Throw them out!

Set yourself tiny, achievable, tickable targets (TATTs)

Give yourself personal and professional targets. This will allow you greater control over your life and prevent you from becoming overwhelmed because you have taken on more than you are able to achieve. We all have an ideal image of how we would like to be, but if we attempt too much, the mismatch between this ideal image and our actual self becomes too great for us to accept, leading to despair and guilt. It is wise to move towards our ideal image slowly, in small steps, in order to achieve success.

My ideal image used to feature a mix of the creativity and domesticity of Miriam Stoppard and Jane Asher. The reality was that I was coming home exhausted and bad-tempered, and was distinctly uncreative in my response to the children's quarrelling. I am finding it a little easier to live with myself now that I have set tinier, more achievable targets. For example, I try to find a short time to be with or go out with each child individually once a week.

One word of warning to anyone contemplating the adoption of this target: other people are not always ready to respond to your target. There are many times when I have sweetly offered my time to one of my children, to be greeted with the response that he or she was busy watching television. Gritting my teeth, I've hissed at the child to switch it off and come and talk to me – not exactly a good start to an unconditionally positive time with each other! If your targets involve others, then you must sometimes be flexible and be prepared to negotiate with them.

Calming rituals

Develop a calming ritual just before key times in the day when it is important to greet your class free of stress. Use these times to switch off from work-related problems. Calming rituals can be anything that might relax you – for example, a cup of coffee and the crossword, a long shower and sitting in the car listening to a favourite tape. One newly qualified teacher I know arrives at school early, sets up her classroom and disappears around the corner to a local cafe to have breakfast and read a newspaper. Now we are not all going to manage to find this sort of time, but it is vital that we do find a small focus of time to calm us down. Even at the end of the day, it is useful to have a calming ritual, which could even be a sentence we repeat to ourselves, for example, 'I am leaving this day at school behind me and I'm going home with a positive mind.' If I'm trailing home from a hard day I try to stop the car a few minutes before home to breathe, calm down and focus on something positive. What is a few minutes' extra time if it manages to save others from your irritability?

Golden Moments

Another calming technique to develop, one which can be learnt and used throughout the day, is the ability to enter into and enjoy a Golden Moment. Free your mind from all other thoughts and concentrate on bringing all your senses alive whilst entering one moment of pleasure. For example, take a cup of tea outside; concentrate on the taste of the tea, the warmth of the tea cup, the coldness of the breeze, the smell of nearby grass, the sounds of the birds/traffic/children's voices and the sight of any vivid colours. By concentrating on all your senses, and talking yourself through them, it is possible to shut out spiky thoughts associated with problems.

I get very worried when I meet teachers on courses who say that they cannot find one Golden Moment. Maintaining our mental health demands that we do create these moments for ourselves. In fact, the teachers who use this technique report that it's best to preface such a moment by saying to themselves, 'This is now my Golden Moment!'

I must be becoming a little too passionate about advocating Golden Moments. Recently, on an Inset course after the final tea break, I walked back into a chorus of teachers singing 'Golden Moments' to the tune of Perry Como's 'Magic Moments' – it was a Golden Moment in itself.

Breathing techniques

A useful and quick way of ridding the body of tension is to learn deep breathing techniques and use them whilst concentrating on relaxing your body. Centre yourself on a chair, evenly distributing your weight, and slowly breathe in to the count of 3 or 4, keeping your mouth closed. Imagine the oxygen going through pathways in your body making you feel lighter and more energetic. Then slowly expel the air through your mouth – again to the same count. Imagine as you are releasing the air that you are also releasing all the tension and negativity.

Summary

Once you have accepted that you are the vital key that unlocks a positive ethos in your classroom and once you have taken the time to work on your own journey of personal and professional development, then you are ready to create positive systems within your class. You must, however, continue to maintain your own self-help programme; energy needs to be renewed daily. You cannot neglect your own needs all term and then hope that the holidays will balance the neglect.

Reference

Burns, R. (1982) *Self Concept Development and Education*, Rinehart and Winston.

PART 2

Creating a Calm and Positive Classroom Ethos

A circular model

Once you have taken time to look after your own self-esteem you will find the energy needed to initiate the following process. The next diagram illustrates the steps a class teacher can follow to bring peace and a positive ethos to the classroom.

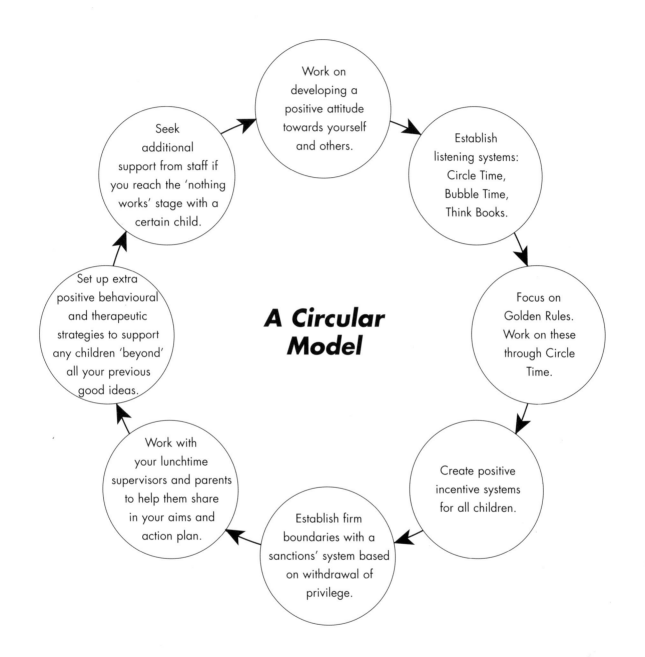

Work on developing a positive attitude towards yourself and others.

Establish listening systems: Circle Time, Bubble Time, Think Books.

Seek additional support from staff if you reach the 'nothing works' stage with a certain child.

A Circular Model

Focus on Golden Rules. Work on these through Circle Time.

Set up extra positive behavioural and therapeutic strategies to support any children 'beyond' all your previous good ideas.

Create positive incentive systems for all children.

Work with your lunchtime supervisors and parents to help them share in your aims and action plan.

Establish firm boundaries with a sanctions' system based on withdrawal of privilege.

HOW THE CIRCULAR MODEL WORKS

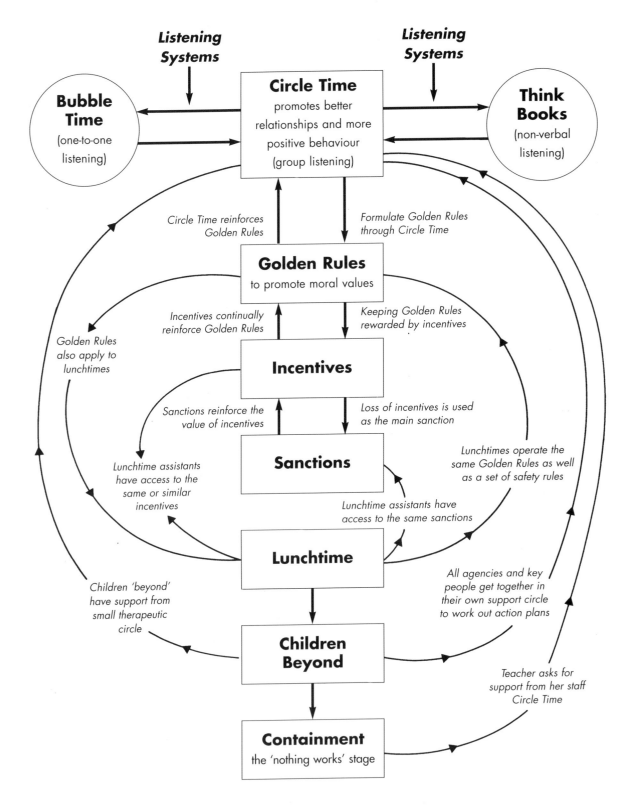

Setting up the listening systems

At the heart of a positive classroom is the children's knowledge that they will be listened to. Being listened to is a wonderful experience, as it enables people to feel valued and special. The cruel reality is, however, that most of us are incredibly busy and our flustered, rushed body movements and tense tone of voice don't combine to make us appear warm or approachable. It is also too much to hope that a teacher, with plenty to do, will always have enough time to notice the wan, drawn face of a child needing to be encouraged to talk. It is, therefore, vital that every teacher sets up clear, acknowledged listening systems. The following system contains group, individual and non-verbal listening to help children feel they have access to you. No system, however, can replace that spontaneous gesture of warmth when a teacher crouches down to hear the quiet whisper of a troubled little soul.

Circle Time – a group listening system

Circle Time provides the ideal group listening system for enhancing children's self-esteem, promoting moral values, building a sense of team and developing social skills. It is a democratic system, involving all children and giving them equal rights and opportunities. It offers children a practical opportunity to discuss concerns, consider and debate moral values, practise positive behaviours and work out solutions and action plans in an enjoyable and fun context which is highly motivational. Teachers using Circle Time have all highlighted its contribution to creating a cohesive and unified group within the classroom that is able to share common aims and moral values. One of its most significant features is that every person in the class can see everyone else. Sitting in a circle encourages good eye contact and our society values eye contact as a sign of openness and honesty.

Key Benefits of Circle Time

- ⊙ Sitting in a circle symbolically promotes the notion of equal responsibility.
- ⊙ Participation in Circle Time enables children to have a sense of belonging to a group they can trust.
- ⊙ Circle-Time activities motivate those involved into a willingness to share thoughts and feelings.
- ⊙ Circle Time initiates collective responsibility for the promotion of self-esteem and positive behaviour.
- ⊙ Circle Time establishes a forum where children can help one another.
- ⊙ Circle Time encourages self-discipline, as each child can identify her own behaviour or work problems and formulate an action plan to deal with them with the support of others.

Establishing Circle Time

Differentiate between Circle-Time meetings and circle rituals

Circle Time refers to the timetabled weekly meeting, which is most effective if children are seated on chairs. Some teachers use Circle Time on a daily basis for fifteen to twenty minutes but, more generally, it is timetabled once a week for an average of thirty to forty-five minutes. If Circle Time has to be missed, the teacher should explain the reason to the children in order to demonstrate its importance as part of the curriculum and reinforce the message that it is not just a 'fun and games' session.

A circle ritual is much briefer and can involve children being seated in a circle on the floor for a few minutes at key times of the day. For example, some teachers need to calm their children down at the beginning of the day. They use a quick floor circle where the children practise gentle breathing exercises and pass round a talking object, completing the sentence, 'Today I am looking forward to ...'.

Some teachers have a circle after lunch called 'Tell a Good Tale' where any child can congratulate another child (not her best friend) for being kind at lunchtime. If children have had a difficult day, it is also useful to establish an ending ritual with a round of 'One thing I enjoyed today was ...'.

Groundrules for Teachers

- You, the teacher, must take a few minutes to calm yourself prior to Circle Time. Resolve to be as positive as possible. Don't forget Circle Time depends on your noticing and praising the various skills of thinking, looking, listening and speaking in order to reinforce them. In Circle Time you, the teacher, must try not to say anything negative. If you wish to change a child's behaviour that is irritating you, you must try to praise another child in the circle for showing the desired behaviour.
- You need to lower your voice and speak more slowly to create a sense of calm.
- You must accept any contribution, however 'off beat', with great respect. Give thanks when possible.
- You must value all opinions equally without betraying irritable body language.
- You must not interrupt if a child is using the speaking object to talk. If you do need to say something, you will have to move across the circle, touch the object, apologise for interrupting and then say whatever it is that you need to say.
- You must not automatically think you have the best answers. If, for example, a child requests help during Open Forum, you should raise your hand and wait to be chosen, just like other team members.

Teachers and Children Need to Agree

- To signal if they wish to speak.
- Not to use any put-downs towards each other.
- Not to interrupt when someone else is talking.
- That a child has the right to say 'Pass' in a round if she does not wish to speak.
- Children who pass in the initial round will, at the end of the round, be allowed to signal if they'd like a second chance.
- Not to name anyone in the circle in a negative way. Instead, they must say, for example, 'Someone hit me' or 'Some people are ganging up on me.' Equally, we must help children respect the privacy of their families, so a child

should be encouraged to say, 'Someone at home is shouting at me,' rather than naming the family member. Remind children that if they want to tell you anything of a serious nature, they should use Bubble Time as this is a private one-to-one time (see below). Make sure that you always warn children that if they ever choose to tell you anything through the listening systems that worries you, you may have to take it further.

Skills Needed by Teachers for Circle Time

- The ability to listen well.
- The ability to be honest sometimes about your own feelings and thoughts.
- The ability to use good eye contact and show emotional warmth and empathy.
- The ability to recap what children have said and reflect it back to them to show you have understood.
- The ability to notice and thank children for the skills that you should focus on in Circle Time: i.e. thinking, looking, listening, speaking and concentrating.

Bubble Time – a system for one-to-one listening

Because children aren't allowed to mention anyone's name in the circle, you are denying them the right to tell you about any important concerns they may have. They may need to tell you the name of someone who is hurting them, or something else they don't want to say in the circle. They may even want to celebrate some good news with you alone. Therefore it's vital that you set up a one-to-one time that is private, unstressful and accessible.

The best way of achieving this oasis of peace is to create Bubble Time. The teacher makes a large circle from card or thin wood. This is then fixed to a piece of wood so it can stand on a table. The teacher explains to the children that this represents a bubble, and that if one child were to get inside a bubble with the teacher, they would have an undisturbed time together.

Explain to the children that they can request Bubble Time in order to hold a private conversation with you as teacher or with another child. During that time they are able to discuss any ideas or concerns. Initially, as with all new ideas, all the children will want to use Bubble Time. However, as the novelty wears off and fewer children request it, the bubble will come to be seen as a symbol of safety as it can be spotted from anywhere in the room. If a child is silently troubled she will be reassured that, if necessary, she has access to a listening ear.

In the early, 'honeymoon' stage, when everyone wants to use it, you will have to explain that Bubble Time can only be used by children if their news, concern or question could not be put into their Think Book (see below) or raised in Circle Time. Once they have decided they do need Bubble Time, a good system for organising it is to issue each child with a wooden clothes peg on which her name is written. Any child wanting Bubble Time can clip her peg onto the bubble at any time of day. The first child clips her peg on at the top of the bubble and subsequent children attach theirs in clockwise order round the bubble.

The agreement with children is that you will only have a few minutes with them when you have the time. This may be during break time or class time. The other children agree not to disturb you once you take the bubble to a certain area. A head-teacher wrote to me recently to relate how thrilled she was with the way children were using Bubble Time – although she had to smile when she heard from one of her teachers that, having put her bubble on a long, thin stick, she was having Bubble Time with a child when they were interrupted. Indignantly, the child she was with pointed to the bubble, saying to the other child, 'Go away! Can't you see we were having lollipop time?'

Bubble Time and conflict resolution

One of the special developments that schools report about Bubble Time is that once children become accustomed to it, they begin to ask to use the bubble with each other. For instance, two children came in after lunch, having ruined each other's games, and immediately told the teacher they needed some Bubble Time together, 'to sort things out'. This is the beginning of peace education. It is wise, however, to give them a 5-minute sand timer, and encourage them to see if they can reach a solution in that time. Occasionally they may request the help of a third person.

Think Books

For the germ of this idea I am indebted to Steve Bicknell, a Wiltshire headteacher, who worked with a group of teachers to promote 'Learning about Learning'. No child is allowed to read a Think Book without the owner's permission. The books are kept in a designated but accessible safe place, for example the teacher's cupboard. If a child wishes to write a special message, record an achievement or write a private question to the teacher she can, at any time, ask for or retrieve the book, write the message and then place the book in an agreed place, which could be an in-tray on the teacher's table. Having read the message, the teacher can either respond with a written reply in the book or, if necessary, arrange a private chat with the child. If the children are very young they can draw a picture instead and put a bubble beside it if they would like a chance to talk about the issue later in Bubble Time. Some children just want the teacher to read what they have written but not talk about it; if they do want a chat they put an agreed symbol at the end.

Example from a child's Think Book

> *I don't believe in ghosts or spirits. My mum said that when she was younger she did the wegi board in a grave yard and an old man came up and every time they did it he came up, but I don't believe her. I think that they told everyone at school and she's just carrying it on.*
>
> *(Child's thought)*

> *I don't believe in any of these things either but I'm sure playing with things like ouija boards is not a good idea!*
>
> *(Teacher's response)*

As you can see from the above example, the child's comment contains an 'edge' of anxiety – a quick, calm comment from her teacher should help to allay the fear. It was probably appropriate for the child to raise the issue of ghosts in the Think Book rather than in Circle Time as it would have had the potential to inflame imaginations. But Think Books are not just for problems or queries – do encourage children to record all happy events, pleasant comments and any achievement or improvement that they have noticed in themselves.

Establishing the Golden Rules

A Circle-Time listening system is the ideal forum for introducing rules to the class. A most important task for any teacher is to establish, with the children, the Golden Rules of the classroom. Golden Rules are the moral values agreed by everyone that will inform and develop the 'culture' of the classroom. These should not be confused with practical safety rules or more general routines or procedures, such as 'Make sure you arrive at school on time' and 'No jewellery may be worn at school.' Once the Golden Rules have been agreed, they should be displayed on the classroom wall.

Golden Rules for Moral Values

> **Do** be gentle, **don't** hurt anybody.
> **Do** be kind and helpful, **don't** hurt people's feelings.
> **Do** be honest, **don't** cover up the truth.
> **Do** work hard, **don't** waste time.
> **Do** look after property, **don't** waste or damage things.
> **Do** listen to people, **don't** interrupt.

It makes the display more effective if the 'Do's' are printed in gold and the 'Don'ts' are printed in a different colour.

A list such as this will cover all the positive behaviours to be encouraged as well as the negative behaviours to be discouraged. The displayed list can be referred to at any time when the teacher wishes to reinforce the rules. It's a good idea to remind the children of their Golden Rules after each holiday, since some of them may have been immersed in a different culture. For example, many children are brought up on the advice, 'If anyone hits you, you hit them back.' It may be difficult for them to adjust to the different norms operating within the school.

Reminding them of the Golden Rules through all the activities of Circle Time after every holiday certainly helps them readjust to the new class culture. Circle Time acts as a primary force to help children really understand and develop moral values, since the games and activities, selected to reinforce these values, are highly motivational and experiential. The children, therefore, are able to understand them more completely.

Be aware, however, that a set of different values from those of the Golden Rules is often practised within the child's background. Once you have clarified to yourself and the children the class codes of conduct by putting up the Golden Rules, it is vital that you too try to adhere to them; make sure that you don't begin to judge children's personalities or characters by their ability or inability to stick to them.

You might expect children to say 'please' and 'thank you', to listen when being spoken to, to wait for their turn, to wait in an orderly line, to be silent on request and not to climb on the classroom furniture. However, the children may be used to a different standard at home and may not yet have internalised the behaviours they are expected to use within the school. Early negative encounters with you, stemming from your irritation when a child does not reach your expected standards of behaviour, can cause considerable harm, as the child quickly learns she is 'no good at school'. A pattern for future failure can be established all too easily. It would perhaps be helpful if you list the unwritten codes of conduct you would like to see in the classroom, then explain their purpose and practise them in Circle Time, so that all the children become familiar with what is expected of them.

Incentives

Incentives are the good news that we give to children and their parents about children's personal, social and academic development. Initially, the incentives can take the form of celebratory, tangible rewards, as these help to spread the good news about a child to other children and staff. Incentives, if used sensitively and with care, help create a very positive ethos in a classroom. Interestingly, as classes become calmer, more productive and more valuing of each other, the incentives needed become more intrinsic. Children begin to see success with their work as an incentive and experience encouragement from peers as a prime motivator. As this positive situation continues and children's self-esteem grows, they begin to be able to participate in self-evaluation and self-designated incentives.

As I visit schools around the country, I see wonderful examples of incentive systems: stickers, badges, notes, stamps on the hand, certificates and so on. The problem is that they are often used indiscriminately, without a sense of working towards something. Part of my circular model (see page 31), therefore, depends on teachers looking carefully at their system of rewards and dividing them into 'encouragers' and 'specials'.

'Encouragers' and 'specials'

'Encouragers' are the small, daily rewards that we should use to notice and re-inforce all aspects of the Golden Rules. These tokens are normally stickers, badges, stamps on the hand and so on. The 'specials' need to be separate from 'encouragers', and could be certificates, letters home to parents, entries into the class Golden Book or a mention in assembly. You and the children need to decide which academic or social achievements should merit a 'special'. You also need to decide how many 'encouragers' should lead to a 'special'. In this way the children can build a sense of working towards a goal.

I have helped set up hundreds of incentives systems within schools and I have never failed to be impressed with the creativity of ideas shown when children and adults get together to discuss these. One class created a beautiful barren tree. The leaves were one of their 'encouragers'. Every time a child improved at a Golden Rule or reached a target she would receive a leaf with the words 'I ... am pleased because I ...' printed on it so that she could write in her name and achievement. (If the children can't write, they could just have 'Well done!' printed on the leaf.) The leaves were stapled onto the branches of the tree, and a gold star was put into their 'pact books' – that is, the home/school liaison reading book scheme – so that parents were informed of the success. (In this system, parents were given informa-tion in advance so they understood the significance of a gold star.) Five leaves on the tree led to a golden acorn, which was their 'special' and a cause for great celebration. Three golden acorns led to a red squirrel (in this class they also had an 'extra-special'!), which meant that they could choose from a list of helping responsibilities or, if they preferred, receive a public congratulation from the whole school in assembly.

I'm not saying this is the ideal system; it suited that teacher and her particular class.

Basic entitlement helps middle plodders

Each class teacher needs to work out with the children her own system which is displayed on the wall and detailed in a letter to parents. The teacher needs to keep a record in order to be fair. In many classes there is a group of fairly quiet, hard-working children whom I call 'middle plodders'. These children neither bring attention to themselves by being startlingly academic nor do they gain attention through disruptive behaviour. They are, therefore, often overlooked. One way to safeguard these children from that is to decide what should be a basic entitlement for each child to receive by the end of the term. For example, you may decide that every child should have at least three 'encouragers' by the end of term and one 'special' by the end of the year. Sometimes, when I suggest this on courses, teachers respond with, 'But what happens if they haven't earnt it?' I am almost tempted to say, 'It means you have failed these children.' By this I mean that good teaching is about creating small achievable targets and then noticing the children's success. If a teacher cannot find some good news to give back to a child, then it tells me more about the unrealistic expectations of that teacher than about the progress of the child. Obviously, in an ideal world, the whole school would share a similar theory and practice of incentives.

Encouraging a culture of peer praise

One of the features essential to my positive behaviour model is the emphasis given to sharing power equally. In the model I promote throughout the UK, I encourage teachers to find ways of giving the power of praise back to the children. It is important that children do not always look to adults to receive positive feedback; they need to receive it also from their peers and themselves. Through participation in Circle-Time programmes, children will naturally be used to thanking one another for kind, gentle, helpful and responsible behaviour. In this way they are encouraged to take responsibility for promoting the moral values of the classroom. I then take this system one step forward by asking the teacher, during Circle Time, to allot a small period of time for children to nominate someone for an incentive.

Golden Nominations Board

It is a good idea to put up a Golden Nominations Board in the classroom. (The gold colour reinforces the visual link between peer praise and the Golden Rules.) Children are encouraged to nominate someone (never a close friend) for a positive quality. A nomination depends on the teacher's instruction; that is, if the teacher asks the children to think of someone who has shown a recent improvement in work or behaviour, they will nominate a child appropriate to this category; if the teacher asks the children to nominate someone who is always kind or hard-working, the middle plodders will tend to be nominated. It's important that the teacher devises categories which cover all the positive qualities of all the children in the class. It is usual for teachers to have several nominations so it is a good idea to have different systems to make selection fair. Some teachers allow the children to earn the right to be the nominators by achieving certain targets themselves. To guard against some children never being selected, it is wise to keep a record to make sure that all children are included on the board at some time during the year. After all, you too have the right to nominate a child during Circle Time. When a nominee has been selected, this child's name, together with the name of the nominator, is entered on the board and also the positive behaviour is named. This is only the beginning of the process. Once the names have been displayed, the rest of the class, the classroom support teacher and the lunchtime supervisors are asked to look out for the positive behaviour that has been nominated.

The following week, in Circle Time, you can ask for a show of hands from the children (in addition to verbal reports from the adults) to assess how successful the nominee has been. If the majority agrees with the original nomination, a nominator takes an 'encourager' across and formally presents it to the nominee with a verbal 'well done'. If the majority decision is that a child has not fully deserved the nomination, you need to make the target time shorter than a week in order to achieve success. Agree with the child that she will try to achieve the nomination within, say, two days and have a brief circle ritual to check progress at the end of that time.

When I first recommend this new system, some teachers feel anxious about the ability of children to be honest about other children. My own and other teachers' experiences of the system show that children, if treated with respect through participation in Circle Time, are movingly honest and positive towards one another. Nevertheless, a teacher needs to be sensitive to the culture and moral development of her class. For example, the older the children unused to Circle Time are, the more difficult it may be for them to adapt to this approach. Then it may not be appropriate to try the system; it would be sufficient for you to encourage verbal praise through normal Circle-Time channels.

Special child of the week and the Golden Book ...

It is a wonderful idea to decide that every child in your class will be chosen for the above title once in every school year. You may choose one child a week or you can find 'creative criteria' that may involve other pupils' ideas for selecting a child. Once the child is chosen, the whole class will think, throughout the week, of positive comments they would like to present to the child. Some teachers keep a large scrapbook covered in gold wrapping paper on a special table with a photograph of the child on it. The teacher starts the book herself by writing in it a positive comment about the child. Other children can write comments and paste them in. Prior to this activity, the teacher would have worked through Circle Time to help children consider all the issues of positive feedback and comments that can delight or hurt. During the week the special child is first in all the queues, undertakes all the special responsibilities (watering plants, fetching the register) and generally takes on the role of teacher's personal assistant, perhaps going through her school diary with her at the beginning of the week, jotting down notes and resolving to remind her of television programmes and all the other jobs the teacher mustn't forget.

... and the Golden Chair?

At the end of the week, in Circle Time, if the child chooses, she can sit in the hot seat (gold-foiled for the occasion) and receive questions about her hobbies and interests and her life experiences. Children really love this positive attention from their peers. Finally, the child is presented with the Golden Book and receives a clap and warm smiles from her peers.

Self-esteem – learning to esteem ourselves?

To help children value their own opinions about themselves as much as they value others', it's important to give children the opportunity to reflect and comment on their own performance. Don't forget to encourage children to use their Think Books as positive records – for example, 'I think I'm doing really well at ...'. Circle-Time rounds encourage positive self-evaluation: 'I am pleased with myself because ...'.

This approval can be developed further by the red dot system. Every week each child will be given one red dot which she can apply to any piece of work she is proud of. She then has to present this in Circle Time with her reason why she awarded herself this merit. The reasons can be various: 'I gave myself the award because I managed to do this work even though all my table was talking but I didn't join in', 'I like the piece of work because I know I tried really hard with my handwriting.' If the child is more pleased that week because of some aspect of her behaviour, then she can draw a picture of the incident that illustrates her kind/co-operative (or whatever) behaviour, put a red dot on it, and present it in the circle with a short explanation.

Golden Time: a whole-class incentive

Central to my incentives scheme is the establishment of privilege time, which I also call Golden Time to emphasise the link with the Golden Rules. Keeping the Golden Rules creates a reward of extra time which all can share together. In other words, you explain to your class that you believe that they are all capable of keeping to the Golden Rules, and if they did it would save everyone a lot of time. You would like to give them back that time at the end of the week as a way of celebrating their ability to keep the Golden Rules.

Choosing Golden Time activities

During Circle Time, brainstorm the children with all the activities they would choose to do and structure them into a large chart. On a Monday each child can sign up for a chosen activity. Amongst the many activities that children choose to do are:

- clay modelling,
- topics,
- educational games,
- playmobile,
- osno-tech,
- music trolley,
- puppets,
- art,
- construction toys,
- computing (this may have to go on a rota system as it is very popular),
- earphones and story,
- garage.

The most golden of activities

The most highly motivational activity is helping with a younger class. If your school does not operate a whole-school policy, it's a good idea to see if you can persuade a colleague with a young class to operate the same Golden Time system as yourself. If you can both hold Golden Times simultaneously, you will then be able to arrange for five children from each class to swap. Five older children can teach the younger ones a game or otherwise help them, and five younger children can come up with work they would like help with or a game they wish to be taught.

Group Golden Time

Sometimes it's appropriate to offer the whole class an opportunity to enjoy an activity together. Some classes choose disco time, drama time, parachute games or class visits. One brave headteacher I know in Scotland offers her children rollerblading time, a short time in the playground during which one group can skate whilst another group chooses a different outside activity. I did reassure all the other teachers on the course that she was on that each must only allow children activities that suit the teacher's temperament, tolerance levels and belief systems (i.e. some teachers feel happier offering educational choices only).

Some Considerations for Golden Time

- It is an ideal opportunity to disentangle a negative relationship with a child, by you choosing to play a game with her, especially if the child can teach you a game she knows.
- Some teachers report that they use this time to paint their own pictures, or make something, and that working in this relaxed way with the children acts as a wonderful therapeutic outlet.
- It is entirely your decision when to timetable Golden Time. Since it ties in with the sanctions system, should behaviour be a problem in your class it should be a high-prestige time such as Wednesday mornings; if behaviour is not such an issue in your class, then a low-prestige time such as Friday afternoons is appropriate.
- To reinforce the concept of Golden Time it is good to put up a golden notice and allow the children to choose some music which they can take 10-minute turns to play.

Sanctions

Clear negotiated sanctions are an essential requisite of positive classroom management.

The Importance of Sanctions

- If Golden Rules are displayed and then broken by various children without incurring any consequences, the message to children is that the Golden Rules are useless – that is, the moral values of the school are useless.

- Some children in our classes lead chaotic lives without boundaries; sanctions offer clear boundaries and a safe framework. Children test their power; for example, at home they've learnt that if they nag for a long time a parent will give in. They need to know that school boundaries are secure and not vulnerable to their own power.
- Sanctions help create safer teachers. By this I mean that if a teacher does not have a declared set of sanctions, children are never quite sure what sanction she will use. This leaves the system vulnerable to a teacher's inconsistency, which can be influenced by school events and personal moods.
- A clear sanction allows a child the opportunity to work off a 'debt', which can then be forgotten about. If the sanction system is unclear, again the teacher is susceptible to resorting to frequent, loud verbal 'tellings off'. This public spectacle can result in a stain on a child's character which cannot be rubbed out.

Golden Time as the pivotal link between your incentives and sanctions system

Having created a privilege system – that is, the children have the privilege of Golden Time if they adhere to the Golden Rules – you will find that it can now act as a strong deterrent. When talking to the children about suitable sanctions, they will immediately see the fairness (an overriding moral value with children) in the concept that if they receive Golden Time for keeping the rules, they must lose it if they break them. In fact, in these discussions the children may be in favour of losing all of Golden Time as a sanction, and you may actually end up being the benign moderator.

Breaking the Golden Rules

The system that evolves depends on the teacher noticing when a child has broken a rule. She may well fix the offender with a steely eye, she may try a 'whisper in time', but what she will always do, before removing any Golden Time, is to give a written warning.

Importance of warnings

Rather than drawing public attention to a child by writing her name on the board, I suggest it is better to have warning slips prepared with the word 'WARNING' written on them. In the case of infants, it is best to have a symbol such as a sad face. When a child breaks a Golden Rule in the classroom the written warning is quietly placed beside her; it is a visual reminder to a child that backs up your verbal warning. You do not leave this out for the whole day; it is removed at the next appropriate break time. If the child breaks any Golden Rule again whilst the warning sign is in place, she loses five minutes of Golden Time.

Where a young child is concerned, the sad face warning signifying that the child has disappointed the teacher and other children by breaking a rule is turned over to reveal a happy face once the child is back 'on task' and no longer exhibiting the difficult behaviour. If she chooses to continue to break the Golden Rule, she can be asked to sit away from her friends on a Help You To Be Good Chair while watching a 1-minute timer. Most infant schools, however, find that young children can wait till the Golden Time to lose their five minutes. Children need the safety of a warning system to choose to pull themselves back from the brink. Without it, some are often surprised by their punishment.

Losing Golden Time

During the week the names of any children who lose Golden Time are entered on a chart, which is kept privately in a drawer. Just before Golden Time arrange to have a separate table in the same room. The table will be bare except for a 5-minute sand timer placed in the centre. Any children who have lost Golden Time will sit around this table, where they will be able to see and hear the other children enjoying their chosen activities.

Sand timers are essential

The 5-minute sand timer is an integral part of the system. Many of the children who break Golden Rules have a level of inner chaos and an inability to understand the concept of time, so they may panic when asked to sit still for any amount of time. As they focus on a timer, the sand becomes a visual symbol for how much time is left and the activity of watching it calms them down. When the timer runs out, those children who have lost five minutes' Golden Time are allowed to rejoin the activities. The timer is reset for any remaining children who have incurred a longer time-out. One teacher working with infants and unable to afford a large wooden sand timer devised a brilliant system. She made her own timer using two large empty sweet jars, one upturned on the other, and the appropriate amount of sand. You can use any other, suitable material, such as salt, working out the correct quantity to last for one minute.

Earning-back contract

It is vital that children experience the joy of Golden Time in order really to care about losing it. It is therefore important to run it for the first week without using it as a sanction system, so that children can assess its value and subsequently have a more informed view of its potential loss. There are children in every class whom I call 'Kamikaze pilots'. These are children with low self-esteem who, when you come up with any good ideas for things that they might find themselves looking forward to, panic because they do not believe they will be able to attain them. Rather than bear the pain of hope and subsequent disappointment, they prefer to 'blow it' straight away and immediately misbehave in order that they can regain control. To safeguard these children from themselves, it is worthwhile making some earning-back contracts which encourage children to earn back Golden Time by negotiating an achievable target of success.

Some teachers have developed this idea further by encouraging one child who has hurt another to negotiate with the victim to discover a suitable earning-back target; for example, inviting the child to play football or teaching her a card game at lunchtime. The goal is to try to help children earn back some time, so that everyone enjoys at least fifteen minutes of Golden Time.

Making Golden Time more golden

I went back to a school which had been running Golden Time for about nine months. During the first term it had been very successful and they now wanted some advice on why it was no longer as effective. I went through the system with them again, checking all the things I have outlined here and all the ideas that would make Golden Time fun and motivational. Suddenly a teacher I was talking to exclaimed, 'You're right, you know. The trouble is that my Golden Time has not been golden enough.'

There is a serious issue here. If Golden Time is allowed to become disorganised or unplanned, or if the box of resources is incomplete and you do not properly organise the liaison with a younger class, the system will become tarnished and lose its potential.

Circle Time as a review forum

Circle Time itself should act as a review system. Every now and then you need to go back to the circle and ask the children questions such as 'How are you finding Golden Time?' 'Do you have any more suggestions?' 'What resources would you like to borrow from another classroom?' and 'How can we "jazz" up Golden Time by occasionally doing some whole-class activities?' Be aware that the children are there with plenty of ideas, just waiting to be asked.

Golden Time certificates

One last, further idea to support the concept of Golden Time and to reinforce the good behaviour of the majority of the children is to devise a system of giving Golden Time certificates to children who rarely lose any of it. This idea somehow gives greater significance to the amazingly wonderful fact that most children behave well, most of the time.

Children 'beyond'

Very unhappy, confused, angry or sad children suffer deeply and deserve – but rarely receive – proper therapeutic support to help them unravel and release their pain. It is not within the framework of this chapter to explore in depth the vastly complex psychological issues surrounding highly disturbed children. I intend to tackle this fraught topic from the perspective of the knowledge and resources a class teacher can bring to bear on a situation that faces her on a daily basis.

In this context I use the term children 'beyond' to refer to those children who are beyond many of the motivational ideas so far suggested in this book. In other words, a child 'beyond' is one who has been offered, yet failed to respond to, regular, empathic listening opportunities, participation in Circle Time, promotion of the Golden Rules, regular incentives to help him uphold these and the safe boundaries of a sanctions system based on withdrawing privileges that he has identified as valuable. Despite all these measures, the child continues to adhere to disruptive or unhappy behaviour.

Many teachers claim they have children 'beyond' but when, together, we examine closely the world within their classroom, we find that the child has become trapped in negative interactional patterns with the teacher and hasn't received his entitlement to the basic positive interventions. If, however, a teacher can, after honest self-examination, say that despite the child's negative behaviour she has consistently offered the above systems and has managed not to get hooked into a negative cycle with that child, then she has arrived at the stage of considering a range of children 'beyond' strategies.

Consider their world

These children normally have a very high level of inner turmoil and a very low level of self-esteem, ensuring that they dare not risk changing their negative behaviours for more positive ones, as they have learnt that their negative response keeps their perilous world 'safe'. Consider for a moment the world of children who have been disempowered; life and adults have often let them down, and many of these children have been subjected to various arbitrary, confusing or outright abusive experiences. They then develop behaviour designed both to protect and release their feelings in order to draw attention to their level of distress or anxiety. If other people fail to see beyond the immediate negative behaviour to the pain or confusion prompting it and fail to offer them, in Rogers' (1983) words, 'unconditional warmth and acceptance of the unique and good person they are meant to be', then the child all too often gets locked into negative behaviours as a way of receiving much-craved-for attention. Hostile attention is better than none.

If you look at the range of behaviours these children can engage in, you find that the one common denominator is that they hurt, anger or confuse people who come near to them, thereby precluding any chance of their entering into a warm, reciprocal relationship with that person. Their behaviour keeps people at bay so, from their point of view, getting told off regularly means that at least they are the centre, however temporarily, of someone's existence without being vulnerable to the hurt which may be incurred if they become involved in a reciprocal relationship with them.

Repetition of these negative behaviours then, unconsciously and perversely, means that they can regain a level of control over their lives and reduce levels of 'unsafety'. Let me try to disentangle this complex train of thought in a more straightforward way. If a child with very low self-esteem is responded to in a warm and positive way, it can be a frightening experience. It challenges the child to take on a more positive view of himself and to consider the possibility of involving himself in a relationship with another person. He then has to trust that this other person will sustain and nurture the positive experience. Trust is a risk-laden response. It is safer to remain in control over your own world by not allowing yourself to enter into relationships. By refusing to change, a child is refusing to hope and in this way he remains in control. In other words, these children have a lot invested in staying negative. Success of any sort can represent a real threat to the control they are trying to exert over their uncertain world. I often see poignant scenarios where good, patient teachers, recognising the deep need of the child for appreciation and warmth, praise that child in front of his classmates, and are then cut to the quick when the child either screws up a praised piece of work immediately or, within a short space of time, acts in a very destructive way.

Let's look calmly at this situation from the child's point of view. Success has panicked the child; if he accepts the praise it means he might look forward to more close contact with the teacher, but life has taught him that adults are risky creatures, subject to moods. He's plunged into a scary line of self-questioning: 'What if I don't get that attention again ...; what if I can't do the next bit of work as well as this because I'm not usually any good at it ...; what if she's making it up? I open myself to the possibility of seeing myself as good or whole; what if I begin to rely on positive praise – does that mean I have to give up my "bad" behaviour? I daren't do that as it has always brought me the immediate attention I crave.'

I'm not saying that any of these thoughts is ever conscious; what I am trying to do, clumsily, is to alert us to the vast complexity of need revealed in the simple situation of a teacher being determined to boost a child in some way and being hurt by the child's rejection of the praise. Children with low self-esteem are desperately hard to reach: their hidden hoping self is backing away wide-eyed and wondering in a far-away corner; their doubting observable self is deliberately lashing out verbally or non-verbally to avoid allowing themselves to hope.

The child that most needs us is often the one who most repels us

Once we begin to explore the complexity of the problem in this way, it becomes clear that success can be a huge threat to children with low self-esteem. Its implications for the child are: 'I have potential, I am capable, I am worthwhile, adults can be consistent, I don't have to control everything, I can let go of behaviours that have kept me noticed previously and rely on people to notice me for the strengths I offer.' It is far easier for the child to shy away from this brave new world inhabited by people he needs to trust than to change his way of viewing adults.

Some children have found the world of feelings such a painful one that they have successfully cut off their own ability to enter the normal range of human emotions; they therefore have no reference point from which to understand others' feelings and they fail to develop empathy for others. A kind-hearted adult, with the best will in the world, finds it enormously difficult to carry on offering a warm empathic relationship when her own needs are constantly being ignored. The child is seen to hurt the teacher's and other children's feelings deliberately. Therefore, very soon, the resolution to offer the alternative positive approach fades away and the teacher begins to make unrealistic demands – such as 'Be good' and 'Get on with the other children' – which are too big and are guaranteed to cause failure. The more the child fails to meet these standards, the more the teacher feels disrespected, rejected and angry. So they both slip again onto the same downward negative spiral. In other words, we are drawn to children who share our own social skills, laugh at our jokes and respond warmly to our praise. We are repelled by the child who rejects us – and yet this is the child who needs us most. Such a child needs us to carry on offering unconditional warmth and respect in order to enable him to believe that there is something good and positive about himself. One way forward for both of us to move through this emotional minefield is to focus on and celebrate small moments of success.

Tiny Achievable Tickable Targets – TATTs

Guaranteeing daily success for a child with low self-esteem is vital if he is frightened to face its implications – but, like any new, life-enhancing substance, he must only be given a tiny bit at a time. To achieve this aim the class teacher and the child need to agree a daily programme of achievable targets. To start with this could be two or three 3-minute sessions during the morning during which the child agrees to try to reach a previously negotiated and agreed standard of behaviour or work – one which both individuals know is achievable – in order to gain a suitable self-esteem reward in the afternoon.

Use of the timer

Children 'beyond' can be anxious, panicky, disorganised and unable to comprehend the concept of time. To calm them down, I have already recommended the use of sand timers, which are a tangible, visual reinforcer of how long they have to continue their attempt to achieve their target.

Ideally, the class teacher should have a series of 3-, 5-, 10- and 15-minute timers to help the children actively see themselves achieve the target set. Teachers who use this method report that the sight of diminishing sand trickling through focuses the children. They are made visually aware of how much longer they have to wait and there are fewer incidents of their panicking and walking off, of bursting into impassioned protests that they 'can't do it' – that is, there are fewer incidents of their returning to their original 'safe' negative behaviour. The sand timer must not be left lying around the classroom; if it becomes familiar it loses its power. Between the times when it is being used, it should be put in a special place.

Once the child has achieved his target, a star goes on his card (see page 54). An agreed number of stars will lead to a special self-esteem reward. It is best if it is not the teacher, but another child, who sticks the star on as it is important that other children become aware of the child's success.

Gradually, over a period of weeks, the timed target sessions should become longer, whilst the accompanying afternoon rewards become less frequent.

It cannot be denied that this whole process is extremely demanding. Many class teachers are daunted at the prospect of trying to find the time for it. I can only say that the alternative – getting hooked into power battles with the child – takes up

	NAME				Total
Monday	★	★	★		
Tuesday					
Wednesday					
Thursday					
Friday					

My agreed target is .....two... stars each day to reach my star reward.

My chosen reward is ....

far more time and emotional energy; and whilst initially the TATTs strategy is a great pressure, as the child experiences success it gets much easier. If you have any extra adult help in your classroom it would be wise to organise the TATTs with their support; alternatively, some teachers, once the system is in full operation, choose other children to be mentors and monitor the process with the teacher's supervision.

The TATTs 'self-esteem' reward

The normal incentives – that is, stickers and certificates – often don't work for children 'beyond'; rewarding them with bits of paper is like trying to stick plasters over a deep wound. Anyway, there's often no-one at home who is even going to glance at them and support the child with a little extra praise. The most prevalent unmet needs for many of these children are for positive attention and to feel more powerful within their world. Bullying others often helps a child who is disempowered to experience briefly the powerful feeling of being able to influence someone else's world. The most potent reward, therefore, is to offer the child a range of opportunities whereby he can influence someone else's world by helping. It is extraordinarily powerful to be able to help someone else (it's why many of us were drawn to teaching). Not only does the one helping get the chance to be noticed and seen – that is, positive attention – but also he gets the opportunity to effect some positive changes on behalf of others, which in turn helps him to be very positive about the person helping him. These children would love to have the chance to help in a younger class, work with the caretaker, tackle clerical work (!) for the secretary or, even better, be asked for their ideas.

Enlisting the support of the rest of the class

The strongest cry received from teachers, when I advocate these demanding strategies, relates to the rest of the class: 'But why should these naughty children be seen to receive extra benefits when they have caused the most trouble?'

The way forward for everyone is to involve the class in the whole process, ensuring that they benefit from any progress the child may make. In the past, adults have negotiated individual contracts with children whereby the child received a range of benefits witnessed by the other children. Because they were shut out from the process, never receiving any incentive to support the child, they became resentful and angry. They had two choices – either to behave really disruptively themselves in order to receive the same attention or to sabotage the process slyly by winding up the child 'beyond' until he explodes.

Let us not forget that it suits many classes to have a 'naughty' child in their midst; it moves the focus away from them. If the child is being told off, the teacher may not notice that some other children have failed to get on with their work. If the lesson or playground time is boring, they can wind up that child; soon the exciting fireworks start. Further, some children learn to collude with the teacher if she develops a negative attitude to the child. That provides a 'Me and Miss are together' feeling. They will often tell tales on the child, confident they'll get a 'warm' response such as, 'Oh no, not again, not after what we've been through with him this morning!' They may even begin to tell you tales when the child is absent. It is essential, therefore, to work with the whole class. When given the chance to support you, they will then see that there is sense in their giving some extra reinforcement to this child. It means a calmer, happier life for them.

Using Circle Time as a support system

As has been pointed out previously, in the Open Forum of Circle Time children are encouraged to ask for help when they need it. The question the teacher asks is, 'Is there anybody here who would like some help with his or her behaviour?'

Initially, the child you would most like to put up his hand doesn't do that. These children are wary of new ideas and will want to wait a few weeks to see what benefits this new scheme might have for them. Therefore, at the beginning, only the children whose behaviours are not extreme will volunteer for help. Eventually the child you need to work with because he needs attention will take advantage of the life-line you are offering. This process is best demonstrated by a practical example.

Teacher: Is there anybody here who would like some help with his or her behaviour?

Show of hands. Teacher asks each child to complete the sentence 'I need help because ...'. Teacher selects child she is most concerned about and asks him to explain further why he needs help.

Child: I need help because I lose my temper a lot, especially in the playground.

Teacher: Is there anyone in this class who would like to help Wayne?

Various children will raise their hands to offer suggestions or advice. The child requesting help (i.e., Wayne) can choose children by name to offer their suggestions. Any child can only offer suggestions by saying either 'Would it help if I ...?' or 'Would it help if you ...?' Wayne can then consider them, give his responses and say 'Thank you.' He can stop this process when he wishes.

Wayne: Andrew?

Andrew: Wayne, would it help if you counted to 10 and walked away?

Wayne: No, I've tried that. It doesn't work, but thank you. Josh?

Josh: Would it help if I asked you to play with me and reminded you not to fight?

Wayne: Yeah, that would be good. Thanks.

I have simplified the process. It relies on the child with the problem considering a range of options and then putting one into action with the support of the class. Wayne decided he would like a badge stating, 'I am trying to be calm today.' A chosen classmate also had a badge, stating, 'I'm a friendly helper.' After each lunchtime, the class formed a circle to give feedback on his progress. If possible, the lunchtime supervisor would join in to let the class know her view. Every time Wayne succeeded in remaining calm throughout lunchtime he received a star placed on a special card by one of his peers. Five stars would lead to a certificate signed by all the class. If he achieved three certificates the whole class would receive a 10-minute treat. When he in fact reached that target, they elected to have an extra circle session with parachute games (see page 231).

How this example fits into the support approach

Basically, the approach relies on individuals wanting others to help them change, and their peers being willing to offer the help. The teacher's task is to assist the children to create an action plan based on TATTs. The action plan itself can apply equally to curriculum or behavioural targets, either in the classroom or in the play-ground. These targets can often be successfully placed in a visual context by using a prepared target sheet. The secret of success lies in enlisting the support of other children and reinforcing their kindness by ensuring that they also receive an incentive which allows them to have some fun together as a class group.

Class incentive if supporting a child on TATTs

As has just been stated, if a class is helping one or two children who are on TATTs then the class also needs the support of a shared group incentive. Don't forget that if a child receives a TATT or self-esteem reward, you should choose a different child each day to share in enjoying the privilege. Other children understand that very difficult children might sometimes need a big bit of 'cake' – but they would like a little bit of 'cake' too! Alongside this idea is the suggestion that the class would benefit from being involved, in a class target incentive system (see page 55). In this way not only are their own positive behaviours acknowledged, but also they can see the sense of supporting a difficult child as his success will ensure their success.

The small therapeutic circle

Some children are not able to benefit from whole-class Circle Times. Their needs are so great that they cannot be met quickly enough within a circle of thirty others. Therefore, they will sabotage or highjack the teacher's attempts to run circle sessions. Check first of all whether this child is truly a child 'beyond' or simply a child in need of firm boundaries as provided by the written warnings and sanctions systems (see page 45). If, despite supporting a child with your incentive and sanctions systems within the circle, the child is still unable to respond, it is likely that he needs the closer therapeutic support of a small circle. Children who have gone deep inside themselves and chosen not to communicate or participate with their peers or who have failed to respond to early interventions suggested previously may also need the support of the small circle.

A small circle can act as an oasis of affirmation to a thirsty child. Let me explain further by putting in a word on behalf of difficult children. If you were a difficult child, wherever you went no-one's face would light up with real joy on seeing you. Most people you met would possess a tight smile and wary eyes when looking at you. This mirror ensures that a child is constantly reflected back a negative view of himself which soon becomes internalised into a poor self-image. Small therapeutic circles can counteract this painful experience as the teacher, with the support of a co-worker, will recognise that her super-human task is to be warm, positive, accepting and affirmative towards this parched little person. If, once a week, a child can gaze into a positive mirror, the tiny seed of self-esteem can be watered, and a true sense of self-worth will soon develop.

Organising the therapeutic circle

As a busy classroom teacher it would be impossible for you to find time to promote this approach without the support of the senior management team. In an ideal school, class Circle Times are timetabled simultaneously and children who are unable to cope attend their therapeutic circle whilst their peers have theirs. As your child's self-esteem and behaviour improve, the support circle is scheduled at a different time so that he can rejoin his class for the official circle meeting whilst still retaining the support of the therapeutic circle. Some schools use their special needs teacher, who has received additional training in Circle Time, to run the therapeutic circle with the aid of a classroom assistant or volunteer parent as a co-worker.

Play therapy

Again, as a classroom teacher without the endorsement of school policy, you would not be able to offer the invaluable one-to-one support of play therapy. There are many excellent books and an association that provides information and resources ideas (see Resources section) for play therapy. Some schools have taken up simple tenets of the approach and offer an oasis of time, once a week, for maybe as little as twenty minutes, during which the child is given unconditional acceptance for the person he is and can explore and make sense of his emotional world through the medium of play. The play therapy method is a safe intervention as it is non-directive and does not rely on analysis or interpretation by adults to children. It basically trusts a child to unravel and heal his pain through playing, at his own pace, with stimulating play object. The adults' role is just to be with the child, maybe playing alongside him, maybe using the skill of empathically reflecting back to the child what he has said, but never making judgements. This book is not the place to discuss play therapy at length.

> *During a play-therapy experience, that sort of relationship is established between the therapist and the child that makes it possible for the child to reveal his real self to the therapist, as having had it accepted – and, that very acceptance, having grown a bit in self-confidence – he is able to extend the frontiers of his personality expression.*
>
> *(V.M. Axline, 1969)*

The containment stage – when nothing works

If you can put your hand on your heart and say honestly that you have offered your very disturbed child the following:

- ⦿ a respectful, valuing relationship;
- ⦿ access to a range of listening systems;
- ⦿ regular opportunities to understand Golden Rules;
- ⦿ lots of positive feedback through your incentive system;
- ⦿ consistent safe sanctions based on withdrawal of privileges;
- ⦿ behavioural support through the TATTs self-esteem system;
- ⦿ therapeutic support through small-group work and one-to-one interventions;
- ⦿ continuous liaison with any supportive adults in his life;
- ⦿ liaison with any specialised external agencies;

and still nothing works, then you can truly say to yourself that you have done your very best given the circumstances. Now, for your own and the other children's sanity, you need to go back to your staff circle and ask if they will give you all a break from that child, at least once a day. Together you need to draw up a timetable within which you and your class get a break every day – whilst the child is occupied for at least an hour elsewhere. During this period the senior management need to be lobbying to get that child to a centre where his needs can be met. They, too, will need all the support they can get during this fraught process.

This is not failure; keep the situation in perspective. It is not possible to meet every child's needs within the school system; your child probably needs the support of a small therapeutic community. The cruel truth is that there are very few centres of therapeutic excellence for deeply unhappy children and we should all be joining forces to create pressure on the government to remedy this situation. Young Minds is an excellent association in this respect (see Resources section). A school's initial responsibility is to the mental and physical safety of the majority; later its staff can put energy into fighting the battle for children with mental health problems.

You have not failed

Some teachers feel that by admitting they have a child they cannot help, somehow they have failed. If you have followed the circular model outlined in this book, you will know this is not true. Your task is how to find the energy to teach your class with as much enthusiasm and warmth for the model as you can muster.

You also need to make sure that you put more effort into looking after your own self-esteem (see Part One). If you fail to do this, you could let this situation, with one unhappy child, totally distort your perspective on life. You could begin to take it personally and feel a failure. All these emotions can translate themselves into physical stress; the teaching profession has been known to lose wonderful teachers because of one disturbed child. You owe it to yourself, your family and the twenty-nine or so other children in your class to ensure that you do not allow your self-esteem to be eroded.

References

Axline, V.M. (1969) *Play Therapy*, Penguin Books.

Rogers, C.R. (1983) *Freedom to Learn for the Eighties,* London, Toronto: Charles E. Merrill Publishing Company.

Helping your children enjoy happier lunchtimes

We need to remember that schools are responsible for a child's whole day. We, the teachers, cannot ignore our role in helping children to be happier at lunchtimes. This period plays a pivotal role in determining a child's attitude to school. Ideally, your school should have a lunchtime policy incorporated into its whole-school self-esteem and positive behaviour policy. If this is not the case in your school, you can still do much to improve the quality of this time, help it run more smoothly, and reduce the number of verbal and physical attacks you hear about after lunch, when the children queue up to tell you tales.

Getting to know each other

It would be helpful to spend some time and care in creating positive relationships with your midday supervisors. If a specific lunchtime supervisor has been nominated to look after your class during wet playtimes, it is a good idea to ask her if she'd mind if you displayed a photograph of her or a child's portrait of her in the classroom, under the title 'Our Dinner Lady' (or, of course, 'Man'). An additional special touch is to place a large envelope below the photograph into which children can put notes relating their personal items of news or giving any comments and queries for the midday supervisor to collect and read. She, in turn, can pop notes back into this improvised post-box in response or she can use the system if she would like to ask a question or to congratulate them.

Communicating well

Your midday supervisor would appreciate it if you would provide her with a list of the names of all your children, together with any useful specific information relating to individual children – for example, physical conditions, illness and change in circumstances. It is also important to inform your midday supervisor if any child is experiencing a particular problem and is in need of extra support and consideration. This can be done without divulging any details of a personal or confidential nature. Midday supervisors also greatly appreciate it if you make sure that they are properly informed about any items in the classroom which the children are allowed or not allowed to touch if they are inside during a wet lunchtime – a list on the wall is most useful. Try to spend some time with the supervisor discussing wet playtimes; and make sure that the wet lunchtime box contains sufficient and varied activities, and that these are occasionally changed to provide new items of interest.

Invitation to Circle Time

Circle-Time meetings provide the ideal forum to discuss table manners and appropriate behaviour at lunchtimes. It will be helpful if your midday supervisor were invited to join in the circle on some occasions. This would enhance her status and allow both her and the children to see each other in a different light. She would also learn more about individual children, their strengths and needs during the Circle-Time discussions.

Helping children through Circle Time

If any child persistently misbehaves during lunchtimes, at the instigation of the child this could be discussed during a circle session. Children could ask for help at lunchtime. They might decide to try a TATT at lunchtimes and to make a badge to wear which advertises this fact.

Examples

The child undertakes to make a special effort to attain this target during the following week with the incentive that if she reaches the target on perhaps four out of the five days, she will receive a reward from the class – for example, a certificate, a special responsibility or extra playtime for the whole class. After lunch on the fifth day, a brief circle session is held, to which the midday supervisor is invited, to review how the child has performed. If she has reached her target, she is rewarded and the target is extended to a 2-week period.

If, however, the child has not managed to reach the target, it should be reduced for the following week. This might be achieved by dividing each lunchtime into four equal-length sessions, the target being to behave well for three out of the four sessions every day. Bear in mind that this child may be at the child 'beyond' stage at lunchtimes and may therefore need the support of Circle-Time meetings focused on this situation.

Teaching playground games

Ideally you should try to teach the children a selection of playground games in PE. There are many good, inexpensive books available, which detail a wide variety of outdoor games (see Resources section). If you have a lunchtime policy shared by all the other teachers, try to persuade them to explore the very successful strategy of dividing the playground into different activity areas: for example, a football area; a dressing-up area; an area for a designated activity – skipping, hoops, skittles, French skipping (these activities change on a weekly basis); and a quiet area provided with mats or seats, where children can read or play board games.

Setting up a task force

Some children, children 'beyond', may simply not cope with the space and freedom that the playground allows and be unable to behave in an acceptable way. If you have a child like this in your class, it might be worth discussing with colleagues the feasibility of setting up a small 'task force' of similar children, with the addition of several responsible ones. Under the supervision of a teacher or midday supervisor, and with volunteer parents or older children to help, the task force is provided with useful work to occupy its members during playtimes. The work could include such activities as making items for the school (e.g. attractive waste bins or pencil holders) or doing jobs for the caretaker (cleaning and gardening).

Take responsibility

At the end of the morning, prior to lunchtime, try to send children to the dining hall very promptly; it causes huge aggravation if you don't. Also, at the end of each lunchtime you must endeavour to collect your class promptly from their supervisors. Being late causes the children to become unsettled, and can alienate the supervisor and sabotage relationships. Don't opt out of supporting your lunchtime supervisor; she has a difficult, demanding job, and you will all benefit if you explore ways of working in partnership.

Working with the parents

From the outset we need to include parents in all aspects of our class systems. Whilst some parents look forward with a positive attitude to school visits and conversations with you, their child's teacher, for others it is a daunting and fraught prospect. It's important therefore, from the outset, to check your own attitude to parents.

Look at the following questions and consider your responses to each.

- Can I find something to like about every parent?
- Do I secretly harbour a strong degree of reservation or dislike towards a few parents?
- Am I concerned to communicate with every parent?
- Do I put myself out by making a special effort to greet or talk to parents when they bring or fetch their children?
- Do I show genuine empathy for all parents' concerns about their children?
- Do I give a warm, consistent welcome to every parent?
- Do I feel irritable towards certain parents because of their children's behaviour?
- Do I try to avoid certain parents?
- Do I talk down to any of the parents?
- Do I add to the pressures of some parents by placing on them the blame for their children's behaviour?

If you wish to gain a positive attitude and co-operation from parents in the education of their children, it is important to establish good relationships with them. Bearing in mind that some parents have a negative attitude to education in general because of their own unhappy experiences of school and that some will be either daunted by or hostile towards teachers, it is vital that contact between teachers and parents is thought through as part of a careful, preplanned strategy.

Establishing positive relationships

Most parents like to hear good news about their children, so try to ensure that every child regularly takes home congratulatory items such as stickers and well-done stationery. To do this you will need to create opportunities for some children to succeed. You should focus on good aspects of every child's work and behaviour when parents visit the school in order to add a degree of balance to any negative feedback you may have to give. If parents trust you to notice the good in their children, they are more likely to trust you when you need to focus on the bad news.

The best way of promoting the goodwill and co-operation of parents is to encourage them to be partners with you in the education of their children. Involving them – as much as is possible and practical – in policy-making and keeping them informed either verbally or through written notes of systems used within your class or the school and any new decisions or practices helps them to feel part of the school. You can show that you are friendly and approachable by occasionally making time to chat in an informal way, either when they bring or collect their children. This may well give you an opportunity to talk to parents with whom you might otherwise have little contact. These friendly moments can be especially helpful with those parents who feel intimidated by teachers or who are defensive and prickly.

Parents will be more willing to support you if you can avoid taking on the role of the expert when discussing their children with them. Appealing to them for their ideas, knowledge and expertise will enhance their self-esteem and make them more open to any suggestions you might put forward.

Include parents and gain their support when creating any contracts with individual children to promote better behaviour. That will increase the chances of achieving success and provide you with the opportunity to discuss with them what might be a realistic and suitable home-based incentive. For example, the parent might agree to play a game with the child if he has entered the TATT scheme with you.

Remembering to thank parents personally for any effort they have made in encouraging a positive attitude, behaviour or skill in their child is a small gesture that can have very positive consequences. Parents are more likely to work with you in the future if they feel their efforts are noticed and appreciated.

Try to avoid any tendency to be judgemental in your attitude and approach to parents – however difficult that might be – as it will immediately communicate itself and make them defensive and unwilling to co-operate. It is important to remember that many parents may be suffering from low self-esteem with all its associated problems. A judgemental approach will only serve to diminish their self-image further and precipitate a 'flight or fight' reaction – they'll become withdrawn or aggressive. If you think that you are inclined to allow personal judgements to influence your manner, it would be helpful to learn and practise the following skills.

Creating a Positive Meeting

- Help parents relax initially with some neutral chat. You could ask them about their own schooldays, how their other children are, how things are at home.
- Check out your body language to make sure that it is welcoming and not intimidating. Smile and greet each parent and sit in a relaxed manner. Make good eye contact, listen carefully to what they have to say, don't interrupt and always acknowledge their remarks and feelings.
- Ask parents for their opinions about how their child is doing. Does their child seem to have any problems at school? Are they happy with what's going on in school? Is there any more support or information they would like from you?
- A telling answer can be elicited when you ask parents what the good qualities they have noticed in their child are. If they can't say anything positive, that helps you to appreciate the pressures both the child and the parent are up against. You may be the only person who can break the negative pattern.
- Most importantly, you must try to empathise with parents' opinions, attitudes, anxieties and problems and attempt to understand their world. The more you can involve parents and engage their support, the greater will be your success in educating their children. Sometimes I hear the muffled protest from teachers, 'But I'm not a social worker.' I do realise this; nevertheless some parents are suffering and their own need is so great that they are unable to parent their child satisfactorily. Teachers are not required to take the full task on themselves, but they can at least have to

hand a list of national and local organisations and individuals whose expertise can help. Apart from checking what the local social services department can offer, they can find out what self-help organisations are listed by the local library. The British Association of Counselling publishes an excellent resource directory which is updated each year (see Resources section).

Ask them in

One final idea a teacher can adopt to encourage parents is to ask them into Circle Times and Golden Times. It really helps some parents to participate in class Circle Times – they learn to listen to children and to value their ideas and innate qualities – you can break the negative pattern they may have become trapped in. Also you can be seen acting as a good role model. Participating in Golden Times by offering to play games and so on helps parents learn and develop a range of skills that could be lacking because of their own childhood.

PART 3

Exploring Circle Time Further

Some theoretical underpinnings of Circle Time

I have to admit that for many years I have never challenged myself to explore the historical, psychological, sociological or philosophical theories that could explain or inform my understanding of why my Circle Times were so successful. I felt happy enough just knowing they worked! Gradually, however, through my own personal and professional development, I started to question the reasons why Circle Time was so powerful a vehicle for change and I began to make a range of connections between various schools of thought. As time progressed I started to appreciate exactly how vast and rich a seam of ideas was available for mining. I entered this mining process seriously whilst studying for my Master's degree in the early 1980s and, since then, I have been extremely fortunate to continue the journey, often in the company of my own MEd students, many of whom now also share my passionate enthusiasm for Circle Time. It is not within the scope of this practical manual to present you with a full array of discoveries. Nevertheless, to give you a feel for some of the key schools of thought, I will attempt a brief sketch.

People often ask, 'But where exactly did Circle Time originate?' – an impossible question to answer. The circle has always been a symbol of unity, healing and power. Many cultures have roots in the problem-solving, goal-achieving potential of the symbolic circle. The North American Indians used to sit in a circle with their talking object, often a feather or a pipe. Whoever was talking whilst holding the object would not have his train of thought interrupted by others in the circle. Anglo-Saxon monks used to meet in a moot circle to discuss and debate issues affecting their way of life; hence we have the term 'moot point', meaning an unsettled question. Many other examples exist. No single hero-innovator can emerge as the circle is deeply embedded in the history of mankind.

Moreno is, however, the acknowledged forefather of all active groupwork approaches. Dr J.L. Moreno (1934, 1946) was solely responsible for developing the methods of sociometry, psychodrama and sociodrama which have directly influenced all experiential groupwork programmes. Whilst the UK has failed to explore the significance of his contribution to education, America has always acknowledged him as 'a great educator–therapist who has been, both directly, as well as indirectly through his students, an equally profound contributor to educational theory and practice and the pioneer of systematic training in human relationships' (Haas, 1949, pp. viii–ix).

Moreno himself talks about his early work with children, when, at the turn of the century, he used to bring children into groups as a 'crusade of children for themselves, for a society of their own ages and their own rights' (Moreno, 1946, p. 3).

It is Moreno's understanding of the importance of 'the group' and of social interaction to the development of self that makes his work so relevant to the debate as to why Circle Time has the power to contribute to self-concept. Moreno viewed human beings as responsible for their own actions, and believed that their natural spontaneity and creativity could, through the medium of drama, free them to direct their lives in more satisfying ways: 'spontaneity as a creative function endeavours to create the self and an adequate environment for it' (Moreno, 1946, p. 101).

My model of Circle Time draws heavily on a range of drama approaches. I, too, believe that the drama process – with its unique potential to encourage spontaneity, creativity, imagination, non-verbal communication, fun and reflection – has the potential to help participants to understand their current situations and liberate them sufficiently to perceive new possibilities and then develop the personal power needed to bring about the changes they wish to make.

Burns (1979, 1982), a major researcher into self-concept development, defines it as 'that individual and exceedingly personal, dynamic and evaluative picture which each person develops' (Burns, 1979, p. 1). The power of Circle Time to enhance self-esteem and help people feel more positive about themselves needs to be discussed within the firm theoretical frameworks offered by Mead (1934) and Rogers (1951, 1983). As Circle Time is a social process, symbolic interactionist theory is of major importance, for it specifically describes the self as a social entity formed by appraisal from others. The acknowledged forefather, G.H. Mead (1934), argued that there are two general stages responsible for full development of self:

> The first stage the individual self is constituted simply by an organisation of the particular attitudes of other individuals towards himself ... but at second stage ... also by an organisation of the social attitudes of the generalised other or the social group as a whole to which he belongs (Mead, 1934, p. 158).

Mead suggested that the behaviour of the individual can only be understood in terms of a social dynamic and therefore the individual act can only be comprehended as part of a whole. Circle-Time strategies are designed to help individuals understand their behaviour and the response of other people towards it. They offer a model of helping that acknowledges that as the behaviour of an individual child is embedded in the social interactions of her class group, it needs to be the class group that works with her to help her become aware of the range of other responses she could choose from. Essential to Mead's contribution is the assertion that the self cannot be reorganised or reconstituted into a more positive one without altering the social relations of the self to others. Circle Time fulfils this criterion because the group – in Mead's term, the 'generalised other' – is bound by groundrules based on respect, valuing and reflecting back to participants a positive reflection of their selves. Their opinions are listened to, their contributions are acted upon, their qualities and strengths are celebrated within a forum that will not tolerate any negativity or put-downs. Circle Times, Open Forums, drama approaches, rounds and role play are all part of a repertoire of strategies designed to help children experience themselves as creative agents within their own world. Mead's logic is unerring; it is only when individuals can 'take on' and understand the attitudes of others that they can regain control over their own situations. Within Circle Time every child experiences the success involved in the activities of initiating, reflecting and contributing. In other words, they are experiencing new opportunities for creating a different, more empathic, powerful and controlled self.

It is only recently that contemporary social psychologists have acknowledged the powerful human need to enhance self-esteem.

> A vast amount of research has had to be reinterpreted in terms of a motive to manage self-image. The cause of these dramatic changes lies in the fact that experiments designed to test a particular theoretical proposition produced dramatically different results when individuals were performing tasks or expressing opinions in 'public' versus 'private' (Hales, 1985, pp. 227–8).

Hales (1985) claimed that self-confidence is the key to self-esteem, and suggests that on the basis of Mead's symbolic interactionist model not only should we include definite procedures designed to boost self-concept, but we should also concentrate on helping children directly achieve the skills of communication which would lead them to feel more confident in relating to others.

Carl Rogers extended the phenomenological framework and, like Mead, emphasised the importance of the self within the social world. Perceived self-concept underpins his person-centred philosophy. Rogers' approach centres on two theories: that inherent in the individual is the capacity for self-understanding and the positive ability to reorganise self-structure, and there are core conditions which, if created by educators and therapists, will facilitate the individual's inherent abilities. 'The therapist/educator must be genuine or concerned ... must possess unconditional positive regard ... and experience an empathic understanding of the client's internal frame of reference and endeavour to communicate this experience' (Rogers, 1951). Given Rogerian conditions, students have the capacity to reorganise their self-perceptions and acquire a more positive self-esteem.

Research in this area surveyed by Burns (1982) proves that if pupils are offered respectful relationships and a warm supportive ethos their social and academic performance will flourish. A careful scrutiny of the main features of Rogers' theory gives a clear understanding of why the Circle-Time method is effective. Rogers viewed people as having a core self that is basically good and whole and he insisted that if a teacher or a group 'becomes a mirror that reflects back ... and if that reflection is positive ... then the client will see himself in a positive light' (Landy, 1986). If a child feels secure in a Circle-Time group she trusts and values and if this group always attends to her ideas, invites her to share in fun games and applauds her successes, then it is obvious that the child will begin to see herself as a stronger, more worthwhile and valued person. That, in turn, will influence further positive responses from others; and so a positive cycle develops.

Intrinsic, also, to symbolic interactionist theory is C.H. Cooley's notion of the looking-glass self (Cooley, 1964). Like Mead, Cooley argued that a person's self grows out of his or her social interactions. It is not a large conceptual leap to assert that within this context Rogers' hypothesis is entirely consistent; reflect back to the pupil an accepting positive image and the child will 'take on' these attitudes. In many instances in Circle Time pupils find it very reassuring to watch and listen to accounts of feelings and see their teacher and peers striving to understand as sensitively as possible.

More recently theorists such as Bandura (1977) and Michenbaum (1977) have proposed a social learning theory that takes into account the importance of internal events and thought processes in the shaping of behaviour. They have stressed that observational learning modelling plus enactment is a more powerful form of learning. In Circle Time children are given the opportunity to watch and reflect as their peers and their teacher enact a process based on respect. Later, opportunities can be created for children to observe role plays where they, and their peers, try out different calmer responses to bullying, persuasion or harassment. With great relief, they begin to understand that there are alternative ways of responding to difficult situations.

In the Open Forum phase of Circle Time, children are encouraged to offer help in the form of 'Would it help if I ...' or 'Would it help if you ...'. This strategy gives the opportunity for children to offer a form of feedback gently. When a child says to another, 'Would it help if you didn't call him names first/stopped hacking at football/started to ask people if you can join in their games?', these suggestions are all a way of giving feedback without blame or pressure. The recipient is encouraged to listen and then give a considered response, for example, 'I have tried that before but ...' or 'I've not thought of that before.' The central place of regular peer group feedback in Circle Time is consistent with contemporary thought – 'The effectiveness of verbal feedback in producing changes is supported by research findings ... and is generally considered essential to the learning process' (Burns, 1982, p. 377).

Glasser's (1965, 1967a and b, 1985) contribution is very significant to the area of Circle Time. He explicitly states that class groups should meet regularly as they 'need to experience the strength that is gained when knowledge is shared and communicated' (1985, p. 245). Like Rogers, Glasser believed that schools often fail to foster 'warm constructive relationships essential for success' (Glasser, 1967b, p. 205). He therefore proposed that the classroom-meeting model could bring back a commitment to interpersonal relationships by creating an atmosphere that is non-competitive, honest and openly sharing.

The non-competitive aspect of Circle Time is certainly vital. It offers children a chance to relax away from academic pressures in a forum in which each child is as talented as every other child in the field of human relationships. Yet, as Burns summed up in his wide-ranging review of self-concept, programmes that 'guide pupils and teachers towards a better understanding of themselves and their interpersonal relationships are rare' (Burns, 1979, p. 310). Nearly twenty years later it is exciting to report that Circle-Time programmes are now flourishing in thousands of schools – the present task is to ensure that these reveal a commitment to quality.

References

Bandura, A. (1977) *Social Learning Theory*, NY: Prentice Hall.

Burns, R. (1979) *The Self Concept*, London: Longman.

Burns, R. (1982) *Self Concept Development and Education*, London: Holt Saunders.

Cooley, C.H. (1964) *Human Nature and the Social Order*, NY: Schocken.

Glasser, W. (1965) *Reality Therapy*, NY: Harper & Row.

Glasser, W. (1967a) *Schools Without Failure*, NY: Harper Compton Books.

Glasser, W. (1967b), in Joyce, B. and Weil, M. (1986), *Models of Teaching* (3rd edn), NY: Prentice Hall.

Glasser, W. (1985) *Theory Into Practice*, Autumn, XXIV, No. 4, pp. 241–6.

Haas, R. (1949) *Psychodrama and Sociodrama in American Education*, NY: Beacon House.

Hales, S. (ed.) (1985) 'The rediscovery of self in social psychology', *Journal of Theory of Social Behaviour* (whole issue), 15 October.

Landy, R. (1986) *Drama Therapy Concepts and Practice*, NY: Charles C. Thomas.

Mead, G.H. (1934) *Mind, Self and Society*, Chicago: The University of Chicago Press.

Michenbaum, D. (1977) *Cognitive Behaviour Modification*, NY: Plenum Press.

Moreno, J.L. (1934) *Who Shall Survive?*, NY: Beacon House.

Moreno, J.L. (1946) *Psychodrama* (2nd revised ed.), NY: Beacon House.

Rogers, C.R. (1951) *Client Centred Therapy*, Boston: Houghton Mifflin.

Rogers, C.R. (1983) *Freedom to Learn for the Eighties*, London, Toronto: Charles E. Merrill Publishing Company.

Quality Circle Times

This chapter comprises written comments that were returned in response to a random questionnaire sent out to schools that had been using my Circle-Time method for some years. Because these comments are based on genuine experiences of teachers who have timetabled weekly Circle-Time sessions, they are eloquent and vivid in the way they highlight the potential of Circle Time. I have selected written comments, notes or letters that relate to different areas of potential that Circle Time can fulfil. Some teachers kept their questionnaires anonymous, some gave their names. Whenever I could, I have acknowledged the writer. I have also included written comments from children sent to me by their teachers. Thank you to everyone for making the time when you are so busy.

Team building

True learning can only take place within a group that a child trusts and feels safe with. If a class is fragmented or its members are quick to put each other down, a climate that is antipathetic to a child realising his true academic and social potential is created. The first task of a teacher is to find a way of uniting thirty or so unique individuals so that they work together as a cohesive whole. Sitting in a circle participating in its various strategies creates a strong bond.

> *I find Circle Time is an excellent way to 'hold' a class together – as Reception/Year 1 teacher, every term means a new intake of 5–7 children. It is the opportunity to set the ground rules for the class. The signal for beginning Circle Time in our class is passing bells*

around without making a sound – immediately this creates a calm atmosphere to learning. It feels that during that 3/4 hour, the class thinks and behaves as 'one'.

(Classteacher)

At the beginning of the year 94/95, I was faced with a Year 2 class of 18 boys and 7 girls – not a huge class but one with problems. First, the majority of boys created a 'physically active' atmosphere; secondly, the small number of girls caused a lack of choice for friendship groups amongst that sex; thirdly, the class was inherited from two different Year 1 classes, which caused a lack of togetherness; last but not least, many of the class had problems with either learning or behaviour – a daunting prospect!

Luckily, all the children were familiar with the Circle-Time system, and I had timetabled Circle Time twice a week with an option of including it at other times also.

Favourite games have included the 'Giant's keys', 'Chinese whispers', 'Circle stories', and lately the most popular 'Lighthouse' game.

The first term was not easy – there was a fragmented feel about the class and I don't think I, as the teacher, was feeling positive! However, working in Circle Times we began to think about one another's problems and about the problems of the group. The children liked to have happy and sad news sessions, sharing things like the death of a great gran or the fact that they had head lice, to the joy of a looked forward to birthday.

One little boy in the group has difficulty relating to children he likes without being physically aggressive. We had several Circle-Time sessions on how to be a good friend. It was very rewarding to hear from a little girl who had suffered from his aggression previously that he was now being a 'good friend' to her.

By the end of the Christmas term the fragmentation of the class had diminished and we began to feel like Class 5! There are still problems, not the least of which is their inability to listen well – hence the work with the 'Lighthouse' game.

However, I do feel most strongly that the Circle-Time sessions have contributed to making the class into a whole and have provided a vehicle for children to express their emotions, to share problems, and find resolutions in a supportive atmosphere.

(Dianna Mears, Classteacher, St Nicholas Infant School)

> *I like Circle Time because it lets you see the really nice and caring side of people.*
>
> *(Child's comment)*

> *We can interact with each other – it's important because it's a time when you can talk about something freely.*
>
> *(Child's comment)*

Personal and professional development of teachers

It's my belief that Circle Time is as essential for teachers' mental health as it is for their children's. Most teachers I meet are basically warm, good-hearted people but they have become exhausted by the continual changes and demands confronting them. Consequently, many of them have become trapped in negative responses towards certain children and desensitised towards the real joy of teaching – namely, encountering and engaging with the children in a fresh and open way. When I am demonstrating Circle Time with teachers watching, many are exceptionally glad of this opportunity to sit back from the usual demanding interactions with the children and have the chance to listen carefully to the innate wisdom, honesty and desire of children to help each other. They become very enthusiastic and excited by reconnecting with the potential of teaching.

Becoming a Circle Time facilitator enables each teacher to experience those feelings on a weekly basis. It is exciting to sit back and allow children to take responsibility for decisions and rewarding to listen to any whom you've not had a chance to engage with in any positive way in that week. Quiet children often get overlooked and it's important that their teachers are gently reminded of the contributions they have to make.

> *Circle Time has been an eye opener, it shows how mature and thoughtful the children can be and how they can work things through by talking.*
>
> *(Fulham Primary classteacher)*

> *As Primary school teachers, our job is concerned with the educational advancement of those in our care. Overridingly, however, it should be about the nurturing and development of young children to become confident, emotionally stable and sociable adults. We also have a duty to try to help them to enjoy their childhood, and this has become so easy to forget.*
>
> *Should other Primary school teachers read this, there would be*

an unspoken gasp of astonishment from many that another teacher should be spouting idealism. 'Come and visit Planet Earth and I'll show you my class!' they would say. It has become very difficult to cling onto the child-centred idealism which caused me and so many others to launch into teaching. The ever increasing and ever changing bureaucracy of National Curriculum require-ments and the escalating paperwork it brings has changed teaching into an occupation much closer to the pen pushing world of commerce that I sought to escape, than the nurturing of sound relationships I hoped to contribute to.

Jenny Mosley's commitment to the child's personal self-development through her Circle Time model helped reignite the spark. Despite all the treesworth of paper forced on schools, teachers going on these courses are turning to an approach which places the child and childhood first. There are other whole-school development and 'discipline' programmes available to schools but I believe the Circle-Time approach is most valid because rather than aiming to invoke the authority of the adult, Circle Time begins from the child and places the responsibility upon the child itself, rather than some all-knowing, all-seeing teacher. It is essentially a democratic process, not an authoritarian one.

It differs from other 'quick fixes' because, whilst encouraging self-discipline, it allows the child to put itself proudly upon a pedestal, alongside, rather than above, others. The child is fully encouraged to value itself highly, and to respect and value others just as much, and so a stable social community can be developed. Schools hold the potential to mould a society which is, as the phrase has it, 'at ease with itself'. The programmes of Jenny Mosley are guaranteed to help youngsters gain self-confidence, and belief in themselves and their peers.

The introduction of Golden Time in parallel with Circle Time, has proved a guaranteed time for all of us in our classroom community to enjoy a precious time, away from National Curriculum pressures and all they bring with them, both for child and adult.

It has meant a time when I don't need to feel I'm justifying myself as a provider of knowledge. I can spend time talking, playing and generally 'chilling out' with my classmates. It was a hurdle at first but I no longer feel guilty about this! I am convinced it is right for my own ability to mould relationships as it is for my children. And of course they love it. It is an enormous incentive to behaving courteously and sensibly. It enables children to plan their activities while taking into consideration the wishes of others. It means that despite where they sit in 'working' time they can be with whichever friends they want to on Friday afternoon. And because it is a precious oasis in a busy week it forces even the least forward-thinking children to plan their half-hour very carefully.

The feedback I have had from parents about Top Secret Notes has been overwhelmingly positive. I have to rely on the parental view of this because the children never mention them to me. The notion of secrecy and privacy of the praise they receive in this way is taken very seriously. I am convinced that sending a letter to a child in this way is a highly effective way of encouraging and building self-esteem.

The introduction of regular Circle-Time games produces excitement and anticipation. It also helps us to share great fun, again easing the atmosphere caused by Curriculum pressure. Nobody revels in these games and discussions more than me, except perhaps those children in my care with lower than average self-esteem. They know that at these times everyone is valued equally, no matter how 'bright' or popular the child.

Other Circle-Time techniques have proved highly successful. The use of a conch injects a delightful tension into the atmosphere, and the use of the achievement hexagon has enabled our collective achievements to be seen to be growing. Indeed it acts as a symbol of the Circle-Time programme itself. Collectively our class community's self-esteem is seen to be expanding in all directions.

(Richard Wyatt, Year 2 teacher, Christchurch Primary School, Bristol)

Social skills

What helps people to be successful in life is their ability to relate well to others. No amount of academic qualifications can compensate for someone's lack of interpersonal skills. In other words, it is vital that children are participants in a deliberate, planned programme of social skills. In some schools, I hear children being put down because of their inability to listen or look at someone when they are talking. I've even heard comments like, 'She's a nasty piece of work', 'He's a complete trouble-maker', 'She's a waste of space.' These are based on the teacher's strongly felt reaction to being hurt, angered or puzzled by a child's lack of ability to relate to her. Yet if a child lacks a numeracy or a literacy skill you very rarely hear a teacher make any sweeping comment about his personality. This is because lack of those skills does not lower the self-esteem of the teacher. If my observations are true, one of the important tasks a teacher can do for her children is to let go of the ideal image of a well-behaved child (which is far removed from the reality of many children's responses) and concentrate on the specific social skills that we consider contribute to good behaviour. I encourage teachers to break these down to thinking, looking, listening, speaking and concentrating. When I work with children we play a game to point to those skills and then many of the subsequent circle games focus on each of these skills. Throughout a circle session I repeatedly look out for those individual skills and thank children for using them. I also encourage children to do the same for each other.

> *No one person can dominate as the toy rabbit is passed around the circle; children can express their ideas/opinions in this safe, secure forum where no names are used but general underlying classroom issues can be discussed openly. The simple technique of introductions was very helpful with my Reception class which is made up of children from ten different pre-school organisations! The three children with ESL quickly understood what was expected and felt a great sense of achievement.*
>
> *(Classteacher)*

> *The use of puppets has been a great success; I am frequently asked whether 'Patch' is coming to join our Circle Time. The circle games have helped improve the children's listening skills and I always make sure our session is fairly short but stimulating for these young Reception children most of whom will not be 5 until after May. Even the most fidgety, more 'disruptive' child has wanted to conform and be part of our special time together. Circle Time means that the child as a whole person, is at the centre and the National Curriculum pressures can be forgotten during this oasis of fun and enjoyment.*
>
> *(Gish Hobbs, Reception and Head of Infant Department, Christchurch Primary School, Bristol)*

> *It has helped me to make more friends and I am very happy at school.*
>
> *(Child's comment)*

> *You learn to be patient and wait your turn.*
>
> *(Child's comment)*

Sharing problems

It is lonely to feel you are different from others or that you have ideas or feelings which others may not share or respect. Circle Time breaks down that barrier and children are hugely grateful for the opportunity to share their problems with others in a similar position and to feel supported by the rest of the class.

> *In my second year of teaching I had an extremely difficult year six class who had never previously been managed using positive behaviour techniques. Two children were permanently excluded in the first term and the twenty-six who remained were fragmented and confrontational but nevertheless eager to try new things. One boy in particular was never included in the main group. He had a bed wetting problem and smelled. His home life was fairly inconsistent and generally his life at school was miserable. Most of the class picked on him and consequently he became a victim who also instigated trouble. I started doing Circle Time with the class. At first they interrupted each other and did not take anything seriously. Slowly this changed. Children began to come up with problems of their own that they wanted to develop strategies for. Other children would share feelings or ideas and most importantly come up with solutions. The bullied child found Circle Time very difficult to deal with and initially he would leave the circle or the room because he could not cope. However, slowly he began to stay and share his feelings with the others. After a time he plucked up the courage to explain to them how they made him feel when they treated him badly. I remember listening to this and becoming aware that the whole class was hanging on his every word. I looked up and noticed that almost every child, both boys and girls, was crying. After that his class life changed. He was accepted and although there were still flare ups it was never so bad. I would never have believed that Circle Time could have changed the nature and dynamics of a class, but it did. It got to the point that if a problem arose they would ask for a Circle Time to resolve the problem. It was the best time of the week, even if we just sat in a circle and told jokes.*
>
> (Alice Witherow)

> *Circle Time is a sharing time where people share their thoughts and their troubles.*
>
> (Child's comment)

Building self-esteem of children and adults

Continual negative experiences and interactions with others can erode a person's self-esteem. If we are continually faced with negative responses – that is, other people's mirrors reflect to us our weakness and our failures – then we begin to internalise these into our self-image, start to run ourselves down and become full of self-doubt and self-criticism. In other words, we begin the slippery slide towards low self-esteem. It is vital that human beings have a balance in their lives so that somewhere they are appreciated and acknowledged and someone gives them respect and approbation.

A weekly Circle-Time session, because of its groundrules of respect and positive reinforcement, can act as an oasis of warmth and positive feedback to a person thirsty for these experiences. Each child needs to feel a part of a team, to take part in fun and in relaxing games, to be consulted, to be listened to and thanked, and to be praised by an adult and other children. These are the most powerful remedial experiences we can offer to individuals trapped in negativity.

> *Children benefit from Circle Time knowing they will be listened to, some feel 'safe' holding the stone. At one time a quiet child in my care would only speak during Circle Time and then I couldn't stop her!*
>
> *(Teacher's comment, Broadfields School, Harlow)*

> *Corporate responsibility is the greatest 'way forward' – it allows for each person's self-esteem to function and develop without threat within the circle. Positive approaches and whole staff support for each other work well.*
>
> *By the end of the 2 years children were glowing with self-esteem! – A favourite Circle-Time activity was to tell someone on the left, how good they are at something. More difficult was to 'talk about the things that you are good at'. Even those children who preferred to 'pass' were beginning to contribute their ideas and feelings.*
>
> *(Teacher's comment, East Acton Primary School)*

> *You get to express your feelings without being embarrassed and everybody is equal*
>
> *(Child's comment)*

> *I like Circle Time because I feel that I can be trusted by people. I feel better when I tell people my problems and I can trust them.*
>
> *(Child's comment)*

Golden Rules are moral values

Circle Time is the forum for initiating and refining a group consensus on Golden Rules. More importantly, it acts as a review and revitalising system for ensuring that the children keep the Golden Rules in the forefront of their lives. All the games and activities promote certain Golden Rules – for example, honesty, co-operation, trust, listening, gentleness and kindness – therefore you are ensuring that children are constantly thinking about and assessing the relevance of moral values. In our present moral panic and amid the exhortations from the National Curriculum to inculcate moral values, I am passionate in my belief that the only way we can do that is within the security of a circle. Eye contact is vital for trust, emotional safety and honesty. No amount of literature or work on moral topics can replace the experience of entering into genuine communication with peers whose ideas you value and who show they value yours. I would be so bold as to say that a PSE programme could not fulfil its aims and objectives unless it was promoted through the forum of a circle.

> *It is wonderful to work in a school with a whole school positive behaviour policy. Now I feel we all know what 'kind' means.*
> *(Teacher's comment, Moorlands Infant School)*

> *The initial establishment of Golden Rules at the beginning of the year (rules that were owned by the children) meant the class had responsibilities to themselves and their peers. Circle Time was a good time to discuss these ground rules, and the feelings of the class when the rules are broken.*
> *(Teacher's comment)*

> *It has helped me be nicer to people. Circle Time helped me to see why people didn't like me because I did mean things to them and it helped me to know how they felt.*
> *(Child's comment)*

Relationship building

Friendship is one of the most important experiences of childhood. Children crave to be liked and to be part of a friendship group. Nevertheless, I often see classrooms where there are cliques of friends and where children very rarely have contact with another clique. Children are often excluded from the cliques or allowed to become powerful, and in some cases a child may dominate a whole class. Therefore relationship skills are a vital force much needed by children. Circle Time can provide the opportunities to understand the demands of friendship and the possibility of developing new friends.

> *Personally I feel Circle Time has gone beyond school issues to family, friends and people generally.*
>
> *(Teacher's comment)*

> *In our class we have helped isolated children approach others with the questions 'Please can I play with you? What would you like me to do in the game?' This has particularly helped children who find it hard to listen to the suggestions of others.*
>
> *(Teacher's comment, Moorlands Infant School)*

> *In Circle Time we always talk about being fair and not leaving anyone out.*
>
> *(Child's comment)*

Responsibility for others

Sitting in your class are thirty lively minds, amongst them natural philosophers, psychologists, social workers and so on. We need to tap into children's innate talents and their desire to be helpful and supportive. A vivid example of this precious 'resource' we have is illustrated by the following experience I had several years ago in a Year-5 class. One little lad, Andrew, put up his hand and asked if he could have help because 'I think I am a car.' What he was referring to was his irritating habit of continually making car noises and pretending to be driving whilst working or moving about the classroom. (Have you noticed that children with low self-esteem, because they dislike themselves so much, will often adopt the identity of something or someone else? I have seen children nestling under tables being squeaky, high pitched animals; I have heard the powerful roars of 'dinosaurs' and the scraping, clanking noises of 'tractors'!) When I asked the other children if any would like to help him, thirty hands were raised as well as the teacher's. The first child that Andrew chose who offered help was a pragmatist.

'Andrew, would it help if you stopped?'

'No,' replied Andrew seriously. 'I like being a car.'

The second child, a realist, asked Andrew if it would help if he just stayed in second gear. Andrew declined this idea.

A third child, a psychologist, said simply, 'Andrew, would it help if I told you that I noticed how brilliant you are at drawing cars? If you stopped being a car in the morning for a little while, would you like it if, in return, we gave you some special paper and pencils and you could teach us how to draw those cars and we can put them up on the wall?'

Jackpot!

I heard from that school some months later that within a few months Andrew had stopped making car noises, having graduated from ten minutes to a whole morning of positive behaviour. In the afternoon he now held short master classes. Every child in the class had a turn in being taught by him how to draw cars. Andrew no longer needed to resort to his original attention-seeking behaviour, which had resulted in his class identity of 'weirdo'. Now, with his peers' help, he had gained a far more rewarding identity, artist in residence! The point of this anecdote is to highlight that the only way we can help children to change is with the co-operation of their classmates. It is unfair to ask a child to give up a negative identity such as clown or fighter unless we are prepared to help him create a new more socially acceptable identity. This goal can only be achieved in a class context.

> *Circle Time can empower children who feel that they are in situations they have no control over, when they receive the advice/support of other circle members.*
>
> *(V. Horn, Teacher)*

> *We sometimes talk about how we feel and if we think someone in the class needs help we try to help them it is sometimes hard to help them but I try my best.*
>
> *(Child's comment)*

Empathy

Empathy is the ability to understand the world from someone else's point of view. Many teachers are faced with children who possess no empathy; they are unable to understand the consequences of their actions. One 7-year-old I recently met continually kicked and pinched other children, but was totally unable to understand why he had no friends. Many children have been so desensitised by their early experiences in life that they see life as some sort of battle of survival where it is important that their needs are met. They have never had an opportunity to discuss or listen to others' feelings and needs. It is an extraordinarily powerful experience for children to take time out once a week to listen and respond to others.

Only if we raise children with empathy will there ever be a chance of less conflict in our society. If they are passive victims of their own feelings, children will stay rooted in their own ignorance and prejudice. The opportunity to develop empathy is a vital gift that we can offer children.

> Circle Time has been really good for helping children to appreciate that other people have problems, and that sometimes they need special treatment/attention to help them get through.
>
> *(Teacher's comment)*

> I like to help people and be able to understand and care for them.
>
> *(Child's comment)*

Teachers talk back

This chapter is based on queries that teachers made in the questionnaires that I sent out randomly. The questionnaires encouraged them to comment on any problem that they might have regarding Circle Time. The most commonly recurring of these appear below. They are about situations which they were unsure about dealing with, for which they needed further guidance.

Q: **I know it sounds daft, but it's such a hassle to try and create a circle in my classroom. Is there any way I can make this easier?**

A: Don't worry, I hear this plaintive cry many times! Some schools overcome this by timetabling the classes in an easier room, e.g. the library or the hall. But if this is not possible or desirable it is best to have Circle Time immediately after a break so that some pre-chosen responsible children can organise the circle for you while the room is vacant. It has to be done almost like an army campaign. You need to do a site plan with the children, detailing where all the tables will go in order to ensure that you get as round a circle as possible. It is a good idea to chalk numbers on the underside of the tables. (You've no idea how many wavy 'circles' I meet in schools throughout the country – which causes huge problems as some children then can't see each other. If they lose eye contact they tend to lose the flow of discussion and are tempted to whisper to a neighbour.)

   I do know that if teachers are not organised and ready in their planning for Circle Time, they suffer the real temptation of deferring it to another time or putting it off altogether. Circle Time can only become a positive powerful force if it is timetabled on a fixed regular weekly basis for a set period. My own three children have taken part in Circle Times and occasionally they came home and complained, 'Miss (or Sir) was too busy this week.' The immediate message to children was that Circle Time is not really important. More significantly, as Circle Time is the forum for the children's views, cancelling it conveys to them that their ideas are not important. So, if for any reason you have to postpone or cancel it, it is important to give the children the respect of explaining why. Some teachers even chalk a note of apology on the board.

Most teachers timetable Circle Time for thirty to forty minutes. If, for example, you have set up your circle after the mid-morning break until lunchtime, that is, a period of an hour, you need to decide what your ritual will be to signify the end of Circle Time. For the remaining period until lunch, you could use the circle for paired reading, RE or any topic that needs whole-class teaching. Make sure that you have pre-arranged for other responsible children to put the classroom back in its usual setting during the lunch break.

Q: One or two children often say 'pass' and rarely participate. Any ideas?

A: Some children freeze when they're put on the spot. Don't think that Circle Time always has to be separate from the rest of class life. You can prepare children for Circle-Time discussion or rounds by telling them the themes and asking them in advance to write down their responses on a piece of paper which they can bring to the circle and read. Sometimes you can ask them during Bubble Time what they would like to discuss and occasionally you can include a known interest of a particular child. Encourage them also to use an anonymous suggestion box.

Q: I have a child in my class who never speaks publicly and I do not know what to do about this.

A: In my time as a teacher, I have dealt with two children and two adults who were elected mutes; that is, they had decided not to speak again in public although they maintained a whispered relationship with one or both parents. This is a serious psychological condition, which deserves full exploration, and this is not the place to do so. However, as I go around the country, I meet many teachers who can see this condition developing and certainly the sooner you can catch it, the more likelihood you have of preventing it from developing into a serious condition. If I suspect a child is chronically shy early on in Nursery, Reception or Year One, I find puppets are incredibly helpful; I tend to hold little puppet chats with two or three children at a time, as children will speak naturally to puppets. Once a rapport has been established with a puppet, I will then explain what we may be discussing in the circle, ask the child to give his idea or answer to the puppet and ask if he would like the puppet to say this for him in the circle. I will tuck the puppet through the child's arm and the puppet will talk for him; for example, 'Peter would like to say ...'. When the child is used to this approach I will then let go of the pre-circle chat and get the puppet to whisper the question during the circle, so the child gets used to whispering to the puppet and being seen to respond. After a few weeks of this I'll move some distance from the child, who must then whisper across other children; thus confidence can be built up in slow, small steps. Another approach is to ask a child to select a friend to speak in his stead or to write down a response and give it to another child to read out.

If none of these ideas works, don't despair. It is very important to play physical games with the whole class through which the child can relate to others. If that child holds on to a parachute alongside twenty-nine others and 'rows a boat' with them in a magical land, then this is a symbolic action of teamwork. Through games and activities, he can learn to share, take turns, listen and to have fun. Words are only one form of expression. (See Resources section for a book on mutism.)

Q: **When children come up with positive suggestions to contribute to improved management of the school, it is difficult to explain the complexities and constraints imposed by the system, which may block their suggestions. They are too immature to grasp all the issues involved.**

A: It's brilliant in the first place that you are spending time in the circle, eliciting children's ideas for improving systems. I truly believe that if an organisation claims it is democratic and person-centred in principle, it must listen to and consider the views of its 'customers'. I ask teachers to imagine an invisible bridge from their children's circle to their staff circle. Every class Circle Time reveals issues which the children need to take responsibility for and issues which are the responsibility of the school management. It is then the task of the teacher to make notes with the children on concerns or ideas which they would like the management to give a considered response to. The fundamental principle of all Circle-Time outcomes is 'Plan, Do and Review'. This means that it is not enough to go over the bridge towards the staff circle. That same class teacher must return across the bridge with a considered response from the staff. There may be complex constraints preventing the children's ideas from reaching fruition, and they need to have these explained to them in simple terms by the key person responsible for that particular issue. In some cases, schools invite the secretary, head or lunchtime supervisor to come and explain why a suggestion can or cannot be carried out. Even though they may not comprehend all the factors involved they can still appreciate the respect offered and this, in turn, increases their respect for the decision making process.

Q: **Occasionally in Circle Time children say things which I know are not true. Sometimes they'll invent a problem or a story about an event.**

A: The important thing is not to be tempted into an immediate rebuttal or public interrogation of the child. After all, the rule of Circle Time is that every contribution is accepted respectfully and this rule must not be broken because you suspect the truth to be different. When I am demonstrating Circle-Time methods in teachers' classrooms it often infuriates the class teacher to hear a child making something up. I explain afterwards in the debriefing session that I have quietly noted the fantastic story to be a flag of a child needing attention and it often helps to think of a child to be attention 'needing' rather than attention 'seeking'.

As a class teacher you are in a strong position to make this observation and resolve to address the child's need for attention another time, but at the time calmly listen to his contribution yet give the larger focus of attention to a legitimate concern or query from another child. Don't forget, you can always ask a child later if he would like Bubble Time, where it is possible to discuss sensitive issues such as truthfulness quietly.

Q: **I know that some staff are anxious that Circle Time may lead to children disclosing difficult home issues and, indeed, one teacher came to me for advice on the best way of dealing with a child in her class who had completed the sentence 'I wish' during a round with 'that my dad would stop beating me up'. Even though I am a head-teacher, I wasn't sure of the advice to give.**

A: I know that many teachers fear that Circle Time could somehow take the lid off a can of worms. My contention is that if these 'worms' exist, it is better that they are dealt with in a safe organised forum, rather than being buried and later erupting in playground tittle-tattle. Don't forget that Circle Time has one basic groundrule – that nobody may mention anybody else in a negative way. Children must therefore be encouraged to protect their parents in the same way that they protect their peers, by not saying 'Mum, Dad or my brother,' but rather 'Someone' hit me at home. Some children who feel the hurt strongly, however, may not remember to use that filter and may name someone before they realise it. If this does occur, it is best, whatever the disclosure, not to react in a strong way through facial expression or verbal response and to let Circle Time carry on with its usual structure. Respond as you would to any normal contribution; for example, if something has been said in a round, let the next person speak as usual; if it's a random discussion just say, 'Thank you' in a calm way. Don't forget that you can always remind children during Circle Time that if they ever have anything private they wish to tell you then they can ask for Bubble Time. After the circle session you can offer Bubble Time to any child you are worried about or ask if he would like to write a message in his Think Book.

I would like to reassure you, however, that in my vast experience of Circle Time, it is very rare for any child to disclose a real problem publicly. If occasionally a child does say something to cause you concern it is because he needs to; Circle Time itself does not make it any more likely. That same child would find an opportunity to voice the worry at some time during the day if there were no Circle Time. If a severe problem is worrying a child, it dominates his mind and he is unable to think of anything else. Circle and Bubble Times and Think Books offer safe listening systems.

Q: **I've heard from one parent that there's been discussion outside the playground by a few mums, saying they weren't happy about Circle Time as it was too 'nosey'.**

A: Any time feelings are aired, in whatever forum, some people will become anxious or feel threatened. It is very important to defuse any potentially difficult situations in advance, by sending parents a simple newsletter stating the Golden Rules of your class, explaining all the incentive and sanction systems, and including a short paragraph describing how Circle Time is used as a regular means to help children think about moral values, become more confident in their social skills and build their team spirit. A simple newsletter like this should invite parents to discuss any reservations they might have with you. This will demystify the process and avoid any potential trouble. Some schools even issue an open invitation to parents to attend a class Circle Time, while some schools have set up a programme of Circle-Time sessions specifically for their parents.

Q: **I panicked when one child talked about death and later at a different time another child brought up divorce.**

A: These community issues – death, divorce, disability, family member in prison, horrific news bulletins – are inevitably going to surface within the safe framework of Circle Time. Don't be alarmed or embarrassed by these issues or this will be communicated to the children. As part of your own personal and professional development it is wise to read books or attend courses that can help you feel more confident in sensitive areas. There are national associations such as Cruse, Step Families and so on, all of which issue excellent guidelines and simple booklets on how to help children understand the major changes they are facing. Library headquarters also issue headings such as bereavement, divorce and so on listing particularly appropriate and sensitive books for children.

The main thing is not to duck the issue or panic. If something which sets your adrenalin going is raised unexpectedly, play for time. In other words, treat the comment with great respect, give a non-contentious general response and then be honest and say that you would like more time to think about it, but promise to include it in the agenda for the next circle session. (It helps children to see you write it down as it makes them feel safer regarding the fact that you do intend to treat it seriously.)

Very little damage can be done by an adult who is honest and does not claim to be an expert, but who, nevertheless, remains calm and responsive. Far more harm is done when a child is scared to talk about a concern. Always remind them about the alternative listening systems they can use and be comforted by the hundreds of children that write that they love Circle Time because they can share their feelings. In other words, Circle Time can prevent a child from feeling isolated, fearful and different from others as there is usually at least one other child with a similar experience. In addition, you can tell them about the feelings that you have experienced, so they can see that it's not odd to feel that way.

Q: **I did not know how to respond to a child who said she didn't like her skin colour or another boy who said he did not like his body.**

A: Some of us suffer from low self-esteem in different areas of our lives. Obviously, both these children have a low regard for their body images. In the circle it is sometimes best not to respond to very sensitive issues by extending them into an in-depth discussion. Sometimes a child just needs to mention something to test out how it feels to think it and, even more daringly, say it. A huge spotlight on these fragile contributions can sometimes force children back into shells where they will only offer acceptable, non-contentious comments. A sensitive teacher, like yourself, mentally notes the dilemma or problem facing a child and after the circle meeting takes time to look at how these areas of low self-esteem could be boosted, through the curriculum, literature and careful planning of future circle sessions (see Part Four).

Some class teachers need to echo the self-esteem work promoted in the circle by deliberately promoting individual self-esteem programmes for all children throughout the year. Parents and teachers report that 'special child of the week' is an excellent approach for boosting self-esteem (see page 43).

Encouraging tolerance, understanding and celebration of individual differences is an extraordinarily demanding task, but it is most important work for a teacher to undertake as it can affect a child's whole life.

Q: I really can see the benefits of organising special rewards and praise for children through your Circle-Time system, but my worry is that I'm sometimes creating a dependency on external rewards for good behaviour which doesn't really sit with my philosophy that people should be good to others for their own sake.

A: I agree with your philosophy but initially we have to act on our understanding of the psychology of low self-esteem. Many of these children have been let down by people and their responses and haven't received the attention they deserve or need. They are driven therefore to seek attention through negative means and often they have seen their parents or siblings resort to destructive behaviour in order to be noticed or listened to. The first task of a teacher is to break the pattern of these negative behaviours by setting up small targets of success that can be noticed by either the teacher or a child's classmates. Extensive rewards are initially 'flags of success'. As the child experiences pleasure in these, his self-image improves and he begins to develop an inner sense of his own competence and ability to effect positive changes in his life. Consequently, he begins to like himself more and enjoy better relationships with others; they continue to reflect back to him his new, positive image. The need for the previous extrinsic 'flag' diminishes as the children's own ability to appreciate themselves, and be appreciated by others for who they are, grows. Thus a child moves slowly from extrinsic to intrinsic rewards.

Q: I have a child in my class who initially responded well to a target and reward system. He is fine when the rewards are frequent, but when they are given less often he reverts to his original behaviour, so that I have to increase their frequency again.

A: In my experience, if a child becomes 'hooked' on a reward scheme it is because it is the only avenue of definite success that he is enjoying in his life. Most children need to feel the warmth of success and appreciation in other areas. Maybe you need to look at the type of reward this child is receiving. If it is a sticker, star or certificate, for some children these are not enough; they are merely plasters papered over a deep wound. My belief is that if a child is always being helped to be good then a tendency towards 'learnt helplessness' can settle on him. The child loses sight of his own potency as an agent of change. I prefer therefore to negotiate systems whereby a very needy child, if he reaches his agreed targets, can go to help a younger child, the caretaker or the secretary. The secret of success is that he takes another child with him so that he is also building relationships at the same time.

It is relationship building which is the key to weaning a child away from immediate rewards. If people like you and want to be with you this is a greater incentive than a congratulatory piece of paper. So, look carefully at the nature of your target and reward system to see if it is encouraging the social and personal development of this child. Then look in a holistic way at the rest of the child's week to see if that child is receiving good news about himself other than that relating to the target system.

To follow a side issue, there are some children who do very well on these systems and are weaned off with great success, but then – much to the teacher's despair – revert to the original destructive behaviour later. Don't panic; this is quite natural and doesn't mean that your original approach has failed. It probably means that the child has had a crisis in his life and needs the security of falling back on his original system to support him through a difficult period.

Q: **Sometimes certain children in my class try to show off or dominate Circle Time.**

A: In the structure that I suggest for Circle-Time sessions, it is hard for children to dominate, so do first check the structure of your sessions. When you do a round with the conch of talking about things they do not like, are you sure you start with the beginning of a sentence which they can complete, such as, 'I don't like it when ...'? I have been in some classrooms where the teachers give a theme which is too open-ended, such as, 'Tell me something good about your family.' This lends itself to certain children prattling on for ages.

Also, in the Open Forum, middle phase of Circle Time, choose only one child who needs help with behaviour, curriculum or other concerns as well as reviewing the action plan of the child from the previous week.

If you feel that your structure is balanced and yet still certain children are trying to claim power over the circle, don't think for a moment that your Circle Time is separate from your normal sanction system. In other words, your groundrules should incorporate a resolution that if any child breaks the positive rules of the circle he will receive a written warning and then be asked to sit out. This can all be achieved within the circle very calmly without any vocal expression of anger or disappointment. (I tend, if children do have to sit outside the circle, to play an exciting game next so that they feel they are missing out on something. If we continue with the same serious discussion, they might be relieved to sit outside!) If a child persistently disrupts, it is clear that this circle of thirty children cannot meet his needs. He may be a candidate for the small, therapeutic circle (see page 57).

PART 4

Circle Meetings

Contents of Part Four

How to use the following plans

This part of the book is divided into sections so that certain topics can be covered in depth. Most topics consist of between three and five plans. Back-up and follow-on classroom activities are included at the end of each section.

The activities are presented in a planned, formal, sequential way and it is vital that you adopt your own creative, 'free-wheeling' attitude towards them. Note that each session lasts for approximately forty minutes to an hour. You may wish to hold half-hour sessions only; if so, feel free to select activities and ideas that are most appropriate to the needs of your class. I do, however, advocate a basic structure for Circle-Time sessions, as set out below.

Introductory phase

This can include a fun warm-up to help the children relax, release tension and feel the joy of being together with each other. These starting rituals are vital to create the right supportive climate. For some classes it is best not to start with a highly energetic game; instead try a more relaxing activity such as a guided fantasy. This can help to calm the children and make them more focused on the forthcoming session.

Soon after this initial activity it is useful to move into a round or some verbal activity to help children listen to each other. During a round a conch or talking object is used to symbolise good listening. A special hand-held object is chosen – for example a wooden egg, a round shell – and whoever is holding this object has the right to speak uninterrupted. When she has finished talking she passes the object on to the next child to speak. Any child who does not wish to speak may say 'Pass' and hand it on. The child who started the round will ask, at the end, if any child who passed would like a turn to speak now.

It is useful to try to link these activities and to be clear in your own mind why you are selecting various games. It may merely be because you wish to liven the children up or calm them down, or it may be that you chose it in order to build on the abstract concepts of co-operation, trust, enquiry, sharing and so on.

Middle phase – Open Forum

I see this phase as the open-ended central focus, which I call Open Forum, for the circle session. In the following sections certain open questions have been suggested that you may use, but this phase really depends on the needs of your class. Sometimes the Open Forum can consist of your asking if there is anyone who needs help (this could refer to help with behaviour, curriculum, community issues, understanding global issues and so on). Children then raise their hands and state simply, 'I need help because ...'. Their peers can offer suggestions to help by saying, 'Would it help if I/you ...?'. After considering and responding to each suggestion and thanking each child for her contribution, if appropriate, that child and others then shape some action points (PLAN). During the week the child will carry out that plan, whether action or thought (DO). The following week during Open Forum, the class will briefly help the child assess the effectiveness of the action plan (REVIEW). It is only possible to choose one child at a time (more if the problem is a shared one, of course), so the teacher must be aware of the needs of the whole class and share out this time fairly throughout the term.

The Open Forum may not need to be as highly structured as outlined above. During this time, it is possible to introduce drama and role play in order to help deepen children's understanding. Dramatic activity can be approached in many ways. I particularly like the technique of 'doubling'. Members of the circle are encouraged, whenever they wish to contribute to an ongoing enactment, to stand beside the main 'actor', putting a hand on one of her shoulders and speaking their thoughts aloud or giving a response to the other 'actor'. My main concern is to find ways to help people share each other's dilemmas and deepen their empathy. Therefore I de-emphasise the audience role by introducing a range of strategies to encourage all group members. Don't forget that this phase could be shaped by ideas that children have placed in the suggestions box or, as happens in some classes, guided by a more formal agenda which is distributed during the week. Reception teachers often use puppets with supposed problems during this middle phase; then the children will act as advisers or consultants to these worried or wayward animals. In this way they feel empowered by their own problem-solving skills. When, as a result of using the following sections, you feel more confident about your Circle-Time skills, do remember to move the focus away from classroom relationships and situations to the wider management issues that affect children in schools. Schools need feedback from children regarding their dining-hall systems, lunchtime policy and inter-class relationships. Don't forget, as I have said before (see page 90), that you are to create a bridge between your class circle and the staff management circle. Whatever approach you develop or explore, this middle phase is vital for encouraging children to develop a belief in their ability to make responsible choices and decisions.

Closing phase

It's important to help the children move away from the issues of concern raised in the middle phase. They need a series of activities to lighten the mood and return safely to warm and positive experiences. You can achieve this through activities such as parachute games and co-operative games or by making sure that at the same time children are encouraged to talk about their successes and strengths and to give praise to each other for any improvements or qualities they have noticed. The type of response depends on the kind of questions you ask. For example, you may say, 'Has anyone here noticed an improvement in someone's behaviour?' Children then raise their hands (but not for a best friend) and say the name of the child followed by, 'I am pleased with you because ...'. The child responds with, 'Thank you.' This guarantees that some of the more difficult children can receive peer praise. If you want the 'middle plodders' to be noticed by their peers, you can ask the question, 'Is there anyone in this class who you have noticed is always kind and gentle or works well?' Whatever your strategy, see this as a winding-down phase which, to achieve a proper feeling of closure, will need an ending ritual.

Getting to know you

The activities in this section are selected to give the children an opportunity to learn more about each other and get to know children they don't normally spend time with. Children feeling comfortable with each other is the basis for building a team approach in the classroom.

Underlying moral value

Take time to get to know and appreciate each other.

CIRCLE MEETING 1

Activity 1 – Oranges and lemons

Aim To mix children up in a circle so they sit next to someone different.

What to do All the children sit in a circle facing inwards. They are alternately labelled 'orange' or 'lemon'. The teacher or a chosen child calls out 'oranges', 'lemons' or 'fruit basket'. Children in the named category change seats; 'fruit basket' means all change. Without realising it, many of them will now be sitting next to a different person. Very quickly go round the circle, labelling half the children A and half B.

Activity 2 – Hobbies

Aim To help children realise they have things in common with children they don't normally associate with. Also to help them tolerate individual differences with equanimity.

What to do Tell pairs (A and B) that they have two minutes to find out two things they both enjoy doing outside school. They must both agree to make this selection. Now send the talking object round. Each child has to say, 'We both like ...'. No other child may disagree or make a negative comment about any chosen activity; but, if they agree, individuals – regardless of their pairs – may say, 'Yes', to the activity.

Activities 1 and 2 – Variation

Take out one chair and put someone in the middle of the circle. That child thinks of something she likes that she may have in common with other children and says, for example, 'All those who like pizza change places.' During the changeover, that child must attempt to sit on a vacant chair, leaving a different child to go to the middle. Each child is only allowed one turn in the middle, so anyone who does not manage to obtain a seat but has had a turn must swap places with someone who has not. If a child who is shy is left in the middle a set of cards with ideas on them can be used to give her ideas.

Activity 3 – Let me introduce myself

Aim To become better acquainted.

What to do   All the children sit in a circle facing inwards. A chosen child leaves her seat and walks across the circle to a child whom she doesn't usually play with. She introduces herself by saying, for example, 'Hello, I'm Sakira, it is good to meet you.' This child then takes the second child's seat, and the second child repeats the process. Encourage the children to introduce themselves to children other than their friends and to select a different child each time so that all the members of the circle have a turn.

Open Forum

Start the ball rolling by asking the children why it is important to learn more about others. You could give an example of making a wrong judgement about somebody – people who look grumpy turning out to be very kind – and then let a discussion develop.

Activity 4 – What I am

Aim   Fun, ending game.

What to do   The children stand in an inward-facing circle. Each child in turn chooses one positive adjective that she feels aptly describes her and uses it as a prefix to her name, for example, 'I am happy Sam', 'I am tidy David', 'I am friendly Gemma.' The children sit down once they have had their go.

CIRCLE MEETING 2

Activity 1 – Oranges and lemons

Aim   To mix children up in a circle so they sit next to someone different.

What to do   See page 104.

Activity 2 – Pass a smile

Aim   To establish eye contact and positive feelings.

What to do   The teacher smiles at a child, who passes the smile on to the next child, and so on around the circle until all the children are smiling. This process can be repeated using a handshake or hug.

Activity 2 – Variation

All the children stand. One child looks steadily at another. When the second child smiles, they swap places. The second child continues the game by smiling at a different child.

Activity 3 – Round: 'If I were an animal I'd like to be ...'

Aim To learn more about each other's individuality.

What to do Each child in turn finishes the sentence 'If I were an animal I'd like to be ...', using the conch.

Development Anyone may choose to ask another child why she made her choice. The child may decline to answer if she chooses.

Activity 4 – I know your name

Aim To have fun.

What to do The children stand in an inward-facing circle. Calling out the name of the recipient (not a best friend), a child throws her a beanbag which she must try to catch. The game continues until all the children have had a go.

Open Forum

Discuss why it is good to smile at people and to be smiled at. Ask whom they would like to smile at or be smiled at by.

Activity 5 – Fun with jelly

Aim To end with fun.

What to do The teacher explains that they are going to pretend that a green, jelly-like substance has just been thrown at their faces. They are to mime pulling it off with their hands, making slurpy, squelching noises. Start with one child. When she has the jelly in one hand she calls the name of another child and throws it at her face. That child's response must show it has stuck to her face, and she must then carry on the process.

Activity 6 – Who are we?

Aim To restore order.

What to do One child says her name and points to another child, who stands up and repeats the process until all children are standing.

CIRCLE MEETING 3

Activity 1 – Pass a smile

Aim Warming-up game.

What to do See page 105.

Activity 2 – Round: My favourite food (or TV programme)

Aim To learn more about one another.

What to do Each child, in turn, names her favourite food or TV programme, using the conch.

Activity 3 – Who has gone?

Aim To reinforce and increase knowledge about one another.

What to do The children sit in an inward-facing circle wearing blindfolds. (It is always worth having a bag full of old, washed scarves gleaned from jumble sales.) A chosen child selects someone from the circle by touching her on the shoulder. The other children question the chooser to try and determine the identity of the child touched. Each child is allowed one question and one guess. The child who makes the correct identification then becomes the chooser.

Open Forum

Ask the children why it is good to get to know more about each other. Does any child have a problem getting to know others that she would like help with?

Activity 4 – Round: 'If I were a colour I'd like to be ...'

Aim To end with fun.

What to do Each child in turn completes the sentence, 'If I were a colour I'd like to be ... because ...'.

FURTHER CLASSROOM ACTIVITIES

Balloon Chart

Give each child a photocopied balloon chart to fill in. These may be coloured and displayed on the wall.

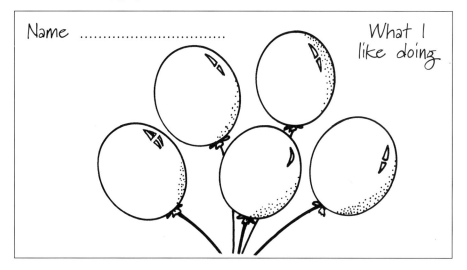

Our Classroom Garden

The children are given a photocopied flower each. In the centre, they stick a photograph of themselves. They colour the petals. All the flowers may be arranged on a large piece of paper as a garden.

Family Tree

The children are given a photocopied 'tree' each. They either write or stick on it photographs of all the members of their immediate family. The tree may also include pets. The trees may then be displayed on the wall.

Note that this activity could cause distress to a child from a recently broken family. Be aware also that some children may only be able to fill in some of their family tree.

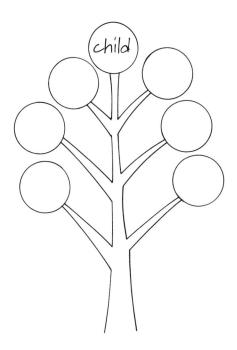

Charts

The children make charts of different physical attributes and write on them the names of all the children they know who share those attributes – for example, brown hair, blonde hair, black hair, red hair; blue eyes, brown eyes, green eyes, grey eyes.

Section 2 – Listening and concentrating

The games and activities in this section have been selected to enhance listening skills and encourage pupils to concentrate.

Underlying moral value

Listen carefully to what people say.

CIRCLE MEETING 1

Activity 1 – Clapping game 1

Aim   To focus concentration on listening.

What to do   The children sit in an inward-facing circle. Each child in turn makes one clap. Practise this in a clockwise and an anti-clockwise direction and try to establish a rhythm. Now explain that any child may choose to make two rapid claps. That changes the direction of the single claps.

Activity 2 – Clapping game 2

Aim   To focus concentration on listening.

What to do   The teacher instructs the children that one clap means sit, two claps mean walk on the spot, and three claps mean walk in one direction around the inside of the circle. The teacher or a child stands in the centre and claps instructions.

Activity 3 – Chinese whispers

Aim   Fun, concentration.

What to do   The children sit in an inward-facing circle. One person, teacher or child, whispers a sentence to the person to the right. The whisper is passed around the circle until it reaches the person to the immediate left of the originator. This child says the sentence aloud and the originator says the first sentence aloud to see how they compare.

Open Forum

When do you feel listened to or not listened to?

Activity 4

Aim   To practise concentration.

What to do   The teacher asks the children to close their eyes and, in total silence, concentrate for two minutes on any sounds they can hear outside the classroom. The teacher asks which sounds they heard, using the conch.

Activity 4 – Variation

Play a tape of peaceful music (available from any natural health shop) and ask the children to allow a picture to come into their minds. End with a round in which every child names their picture briefly.

CIRCLE MEETING 2

Activity 1 – Clapping and chanting

Aim   To increase listening skills.

What to do   The children sit in an inward-facing circle. The teacher establishes a rhythm of claps, then adds a chant to the claps which must be copied exactly by the children; for example:

> *Clap*   *clap*   *clap*   *clap*   *clap*   *clap*
> *I*   *like*   *milk*   *I*   *like*   *cheese*
>
> *clap*   *clap*   *clap*   *clap*   *clap*   *clap*   *clap*
> *John*   –   *went*   *to*   –   –   *town*

To make this easier, the example could be written out and displayed. As the children become competent the rhythms may be altered and more complex patterns used.

Activity 2 – Story roundabout

Aim   To enhance listening skills and concentration.

What to do   The children sit in an inward-facing circle. A child or teacher begins a story which each child in turn continues by adding a sentence.

Activity 2 – Variation

This can be made even more fun by adding only one word each.

Activity 3 – Simon says

Aim To enhance listening skills and concentration.

What to do The children stand. They follow instructions from a child or teacher in the centre of the circle, but only when the prefix 'Simon says' is put before the instruction. For example:

'Simon says put your hands on your head.' The children follow this instruction.

'Touch your toes.' The children disregard this instruction.

Anyone who does not respond correctly is out and sits down.

Open Forum

The teacher asks the children what else, as well as listening, helps people to concentrate. Does any child need help with concentration in class?

Activity 4 – Guess the sound

Aim Ending game.

What to do The children sit in an inward-facing circle and close their eyes. The teacher either plays a recorded selection of different sounds, or uses some familiar objects or instruments which produce a noise. The children guess what they are. Examples are a box of matches, keys, cereals in packet, a rattle and a mouth organ.

CIRCLE MEETING 3

Activity 1 – Where are the keys?

Aim To enhance listening skills.

What to do The children sit in an inward-facing circle. One child is chosen to stand, blindfolded, in the centre. A bunch of keys or some other noisy object is passed from child to child around the circle, as quietly as possible. The child in the centre must listen, try to identify where the keys are, and then shout, 'Stop' and point in that direction. When a correct guess is made another child takes his place in the centre.

Activity 2 – Marching

Aim   To enhance listening skills.

What to do   The children stand in a circle. The teacher or a child bangs a drum and the children march in rhythm in a clockwise direction to the drum beats. The drummer varies the tempo. The volume may also be varied; quiet beats could mean walking on tiptoe, fairly loud beats walking normally and very loud ones stamping their feet.

Activity 3 – Musical daydream

Aim   To enhance listening skills and encourage imagination.

What to do   The children sit or lie with their eyes closed while the teacher plays a piece of music. The children are asked to imagine a scene in which things change (rather than single pictures) that the music suggests to them.

Activity 4 – Round and discussion

Aim   To enhance listening skills and encourage imagination.

What to do   Using the conch, the children tell what scene the music suggested to them. The teacher can ask them what type of sounds suggest certain things and why.

Open Forum

What noises frighten us or make us happy?

Activity 5 – Chinese whispers

Aim   Ending game.

What to do   See page 112.

CIRCLE MEETING 4

Activity 1 – My father went to the shop

Aim To enhance listening skills and encourage concentration.

What to do The children sit in an inward-facing circle. One child begins by saying, 'My father went to the shop and bought ...' and names an item such as bread. The next child repeats this sentence, including bread and adding another item. Each child in turn repeats the sentence, all the previous items and adds a new item, until someone makes a mistake. The sentence then begins again.

Activity 2 – Fox and rabbit

Aim To enhance listening skills.

What to do The children stand in a circle. Two are chosen to play the fox and the rabbit and are blindfolded. All the children must remain as quiet as possible, while the fox listens for the footsteps revealing the rabbit's whereabouts inside the circle and tries to catch it. Children standing in the circle are trees. If the fox or rabbit strays out to the edge they guide him back towards the centre with a gentle touch on the palm of his hand.

Activity 3 – Music roundabout

Aim To enhance listening skills and encourage concentration.

What to do The teacher or a child instructs the class using a xylophone or drum. A different number of beats is given for each instruction; for example, one beat means sit, two beats stand, three beats walk in a clockwise direction, four beats change direction.

Activity 4 – Round: 'If I were a musical instrument I'd be ...'

Aim Fun.

What to do The children sit in an inward-facing circle and, using the conch, complete the sentence, 'If I were a musical instrument I'd be ...'.

Open Forum

Hot seat. Place a chair in the middle of the circle. Any child may volunteer to sit on the chair and explain why he chose his particular instrument. Other children may ask him questions.

Activity 5 – Clapping game 1

Aim   Ending game.

What to do   See page 112.

FURTHER CLASSROOM ACTIVITIES

Musical Pictures

Draw a picture or make up a story suggested by a piece of music.

Listening Chart

Make a list for classroom display of all the things that help you listen and concentrate.

Sound Charades

The children think of something and imitate the sound it makes (e.g., an animal or a car). Other children have to guess what it is.

Listened-well Target Pictures

The teacher prepares a photocopied worksheet for each child.

Suggested sticker

When a teacher thinks a child has listened well, she gives him a sticker to put on his worksheet. When a child has six stickers on his target picture, it is displayed on the wall.

Section 3 – Feelings

This section looks at the range of feelings we all experience and what causes them. It encourages the children to consider how their behaviour can affect other children's feelings.

Underlying moral value

Consider other people's feelings.

CIRCLE MEETING 1

Activity 1 – Five pins

Aim Fun, warming-up exercise, co-operation.

What to do The children sit in an inward-facing circle. The teacher selects five children as pins. They stand in the middle. At the command, 'Pins down', any or all of the five pins may return to their seats, but they must be replaced by other children so that there are always five pins standing. If there are more than five, some children must sit down again. This game can be chaotic to start with, but once the children get the idea it works well.

Activity 2 – Faces 1

Aim To introduce the theme of feelings.

What to do The children sit in an inward-facing circle. The teacher names a feeling and the children have to put on an appropriate face; for example, happy, angry, disappointed, embarrassed, sad, nervous, lonely, good.

Activity 3 – Round: 'I feel nervous when ...'

Aim To share incidents that generate certain feelings.

What to do The children sit in an inward-facing circle. Using the conch, each child in turn completes the sentence, 'I feel nervous when ...'.

Open Forum

Everyone has feelings. Do people always feel the same way? The teacher can illustrate this by using an example such as the following. A child falls over in the playground. One child can't help laughing at the sight, another feels sympathetic and rushes to help, a third feels anxious and stands watching with a worried expression. Children may use the conch to give examples of their own.

Does any child feel unhappy or worried about anything in the playground that she would like help with?

Activity 4 – Musical feelings

Aim   Ending game.

What to do   The children either sit or lie with their eyes closed. The teacher plays different types of taped music and asks them to imagine what type of feeling each piece of music suggests. An alternative to this activity is a round of 'I feel happy when ...'.

CIRCLE MEETING 2

Activity 1 – Birthday game

Aim   Fun. Warming-up exercise.

What to do   The children sit in an inward-facing circle. The teacher calls out any month of the year. All the children with birthdays in that month stand up and run round the outside of the circle in a clockwise direction until they reach their chairs again and sit down. The game continues until all twelve months have been called.

Activity 2 – Look how I feel

Aim   Fun, to explore body language of feelings.

What to do   The children are divided into small groups of 3 or 4. Each group is given a card with a feeling written on it – for example, anger, sadness, happiness – and told not to say the word out loud. The groups are told to practise looking and walking in ways that show this feeling silently. The children then sit in an inward-facing circle while each group mimes its feeling in the centre. The other children guess what each feeling is.

Activity 3 – Can I try to understand?

Aim   To develop empathy and sensitivity towards others. To help children express feelings anonymously.

What to do   The children are each given a slip of paper with the sentence, 'I feel worried when ...' to be completed. The slips of paper are folded in half and put in a container. The children sit in an inward-facing circle and the container is placed in the centre. Each child in turn takes out a slip of paper and reads out the worry, trying to imagine it as her own concern.

Open Forum

The teacher discusses worries and the best way to deal with them. Does any child have a worry about school that she would like help with?

Activity 4 – Round: 'Something good ...'

Aim Ending on a positive note.

What to do Using the conch, each child in turn completes the sentence, 'Something good that happened to me this week was ...'.

CIRCLE MEETING 3

Activity 1 – Word game

Aim Warm-up exercise, fun.

What to do The children play word association around the circle with two claps in between – for example, tree, clap clap, leaf, clap clap, flower, clap clap, yellow, clap clap, sun and so on. If anyone is stuck and the rhythm is broken she begins with a new word.

Activity 2 – John's day

Aim To explore what type of incidents trigger certain feelings.

What to do The children are each given a prepared card which has two columns, one headed 'red' and one 'blue'. The teacher explains that the red column is for good feelings and the blue one for bad feelings. The teacher reads the story of John's day (see page 123), and the children put a tick in the red or blue column as each incident happens to show how John felt. At the end of the story the children add up the ticks in each column.

Open Forum

The teacher asks the children to decide by looking at the red and blue columns whether at the end of John's day he felt happy or sad. Afterwards the teacher asks what sort of things make them feel bad. Does any child feel bad about anything that she would like help with?

Circle Meeting 3: Activity 2 – John's Day

John woke up and looked at his clock. He had overslept; it was 8.30 a.m. Hurriedly, he leapt out of bed and threw on his clothes. He felt hungry, but didn't have time to eat breakfast. He grabbed his school bag and lunch box and raced out of the house and down the path.

John was running so fast along the pavement to school that he tripped over a large crack and went sprawling. He felt a sharp pain and peered down at his grazed knees. Limping, he tried to hurry the rest of the way, but his knees were hurting so much that they slowed him down. The headteacher was walking across the empty playground when John arrived at school, and she shouted at John to hurry up as he was very late. John felt scared; he did not like to be told off by the headteacher and wondered if he would get into trouble.

Mrs Rogers, John's teacher, looked up sternly as John burst into the classroom, but her face became kind as she noticed his knees. 'Dear me, John,' she said, 'you seem to have had a nasty accident. Shall we get the nurse to look at your knees?'

When John came back to the classroom and got out his Think Book, he found that he had forgotten to bring his pencil case to school. He didn't want to get into any more trouble so he just pretended that he was busy writing.

When the children were told to pack their work away, John quietly asked Sakira if she would lend him a pencil for the day. 'No,' she replied. 'You are not borrowing any of my things. You should have your own.'

'Don't worry,' said Sarah. 'Here, you can borrow one of mine.'

'Thank you,' said John, feeling relieved that he wouldn't have to tell Mrs Rogers he'd forgotten his pencil case.

Later, in the dining hall, John opened his lunch box. 'Oh no,' he thought, 'yucky peanut butter sandwiches! I hate them, and Mum hasn't put me any crisps in.' He felt really fed up.

After lunch he limped out into the playground for a game of football. At least that would cheer him up. 'You can't play with those knees,' said Sam. 'You'll just be useless.' Miserably, John wandered off on his own.

'Well, John,' said Mrs Biggins, the dinner lady, 'you look fed up, what's the matter, eh?'

John told her about his being late, his knees, and not being allowed to play football.

'Oh, you poor thing,' said Mrs Biggins. 'I'll have to see if I can cheer you up.' She started to ask John about things he liked doing and soon he was excitedly telling her about the model space station he'd been building at home for nearly two months. He forgot all about his problems as he told Mrs Biggins how he had built this bit and that part and that it was nearly completed.

John felt happier when he went in for afternoon lessons. At the end of school, he collected his coat and waited for David, his friend. Billy saw him waiting. 'Hey, John,' he said, 'David's already gone. He went off with Steve. He was going to Steve's house to see his new puppies.' John felt very upset. David was his best friend and they always walked home together. He felt left out.

When John arrived home, a delicious smell greeted him as he opened the door. 'Oh, brilliant!' he thought. 'It's spaghetti bolognaise, my favourite.' That made him feel better.

After tea, John went to get his coat so that he could go out and play with his friends. 'Oh, John,' his mother called, 'you can't go out tonight. You have to help me. Your sister has lots of homework today, so you'll have to help me instead of her.' With a sigh John hung his coat up again.

When all the jobs were finished, John asked his mother if he could bring his model space station downstairs and work on it on the kitchen table. 'Yes, John, of course you can,' she answered. Carefully John carried his precious masterpiece out of his bedroom and walked slowly down the stairs. He was concentrating on the model so hard that he did not see the cat lying in the kitchen doorway.

John tripped over the cat. The model flew out of his hands and onto the floor, where it broke into a dozen pieces.

Activity 3 – Wizard Wonderful

Aim   To end on a positive note.

What to do   The teacher shows the children a hat and explains that when anyone wears this item of clothing she becomes Wizard Wonderful and can wish for something that will make people happy. The teacher can give examples such as, 'I wish that the sun would always shine at weekends', 'I wish that all sick people were made better', 'I wish that teachers gave all children sweets every day.' The examples can be age-appropriate. The children are told that anyone may have a turn and wear the hat, but she may make only one wish at a time.

FURTHER CLASSROOM ACTIVITIES

Colour Charts

Children make a colour chart of feelings, thinking about which colours suggest feelings. The charts could be done in pairs and displayed on the wall.

Stories

In small groups the children make up a story about an imaginary child's day. They decide whether it will be a good or bad day and, therefore, what will happen. These may be recorded in pictures, comic strips or prose.

Plays

The children are divided into groups. Each group is given a feeling to concentrate on. The group makes up a short play to illustrate the feeling. The play is performed to the other children so that the feeling is fully explored by the whole class.

Feelings

Make a chart for display listing certain feelings, for example fear and anger. By the side of each feeling the children write a sentence about what makes them fearful, angry and so on.

Section 4 – Being kind

This section focuses the children's attention on the benefits of being kind to others and being shown kindness by others.

Underlying moral value

Do be kind to others.

CIRCLE MEETING 1

Activity 1 – Oranges and lemons

Aim To mix up the children so they are not sitting by friends.

What to do See page 104.

Activity 2 – Kind comments

Aim To introduce the idea of making positive statements about others so that they feel good.

What to do Each child forms a pair with the child sitting directly to his right. The members of each pair question one another so that they can each give three positive statements about their partner. For example:

> 'John is good at football. He can run really fast. He helps his dad with the garden.'
> 'Vicky has lovely soft hair. She is always polite. She helps at the riding school.'

Activity 3 – Something kind

Aim To focus the children's attention on kind acts.

What to do The children sit in an inward-facing circle. Using the conch, each child completes the sentence, 'Something kind I did was …'.

Open Forum

The teacher asks the children to consider how they felt when someone was kind or unkind to them. She then asks how they felt when they were kind or unkind themselves and encourages the responses that everyone benefits from kindness, but no-one benefits from unkindness. Does any child have a problem with someone being unkind to him that he would like help with? Don't forget the groundrule that a child must not name another child in a negative way, but must say 'someone', or 'some people'.

Activity 4 – Musical statues with mime

Aim Fun, ending game.

What to do All the children stand in a circle. The teacher gives them a task they must mime – for example, washing a car, hanging clothes on a washing line – while music is played. When the music stops they must 'freeze'. Anyone who moves is out and sits down.

CIRCLE MEETING 2

Activity 1 – Electric squeeze

Aim Warming-up exercise, to generate friendliness.

What to do All the children and the teacher stand in an inward-facing circle and hold hands. The teacher squeezes the hand of child on her right, who squeezes the hand of child on his right, and so on around the circle until the 'squeeze' comes back round to the teacher. This may be done several times to see how fast the 'squeeze' can travel around the circle.

Activity 2 – Well done, good try!

Aim To help children praise each other.

What to do The children sit in an inward-facing circle. The teacher introduces an object and asks a child to move into the centre to mime an action using the object as something different. For example, a ruler could be an umbrella, and a toothbrush could be a cricket bat. The other children try in turn to guess what the object is being used as. If one answers correctly the child in the centre says, 'Well done!' The two children then change over, and the child now in the centre uses the object in a different way. If the answer is incorrect the child in the centre responds with 'Good try.' After several turns, a different object may be introduced.

Open Forum

The teacher asks the children why it is important to say 'Good try' to people, even if they are not correct. Children are prompted to respond that praise encourages people because it makes them feel good instead of embarrassed or upset when they have done something wrong. Is any child finding something difficult that he needs encouragement about?

Activity 3 – I'd like to say 'Well done'

Aim　To encourage kindness and praise.

What to do　The children sit in an inward-facing circle. The teacher has all the children's names in a container. One by one the names are pulled out by the teacher or a particular child. The teacher asks each time for a volunteer to stand up and say, 'I'd like to say "Well done" to ... because ...'. He must choose one good or kind thing which the child named has done recently. The teacher may need to encourage or prompt children when certain names are pulled out. Prior to doing this exercise, make sure you glance through a list of your children's names and are ready to say something positive about each one so that, if necessary, you can be a volunteer as well as the children.

Activity 4 – Clapping game 2

Aim　Fun, ending game.

What to do　See page 112.

CIRCLE MEETING 3

Activity 1 – Pass a smile

Aim　To create a positive atmosphere.

What to do　See page 105.

Activity 2 – Spider's web

Aim　Fun, helping others.

What to do　Push the chairs back so that the children can stand in an inward-facing circle that is larger than usual. One child is chosen to be the spider and stands in the middle. The other children are flies and are numbered 1, 2, 1, 2, 1, 2 alternately around the circle. When the teacher calls '1' all the number 1s have to try to cross to the other side of the circle. If the spider catches any of them, he is trapped in the web and must stand still. The spider then collects all the caught flies and guards them in the middle of the circle. The teacher tells the number 2s that they must help the trapped flies. If they can touch one without being caught by the spider, that fly will be released. If, however, the spider touches a number 2, he also becomes trapped and must stand still. At the end of the game choose a new spider and repeat, reversing the numbers.

Activity 3 – School of kind magic

Aim To encourage consideration of others.

What to do The children sit in an inward-facing circle. The teacher explains to them that they are attending the school of kind magic. When they hold the magic wand (a ruler or stick will do), they may wish for something good for another person. To ensure that all children are included, this activity can take place in pairs (A and B) around the circle so that A states something he would like to happen. (The teacher could give the children examples beforehand – e.g., 'I'd like to spell better', 'I'd like to be good at reading', 'I'd like to have my own bedroom', 'I'd like curly hair.') B holds the wand and makes a wish. For example:

> A: I'd like to be good at reading.
> B: I am the magician of kind magic and I wish that A will become very good at reading.

B then states his desire and A holds the wand and makes the wish.

Open Forum

Passing the conch round, the children are asked in turn what wishes they might make for people in a wider context; for example, family members, other children around the world. Would any child like help with something that is worrying him or making him unhappy in school?

CIRCLE MEETING 4

Activity 1 – Clapping and chanting game

Aim Warm-up exercise, fun.

What to do See page 113.

Activity 2 – Story mime

Aim To reinforce the value of kindness and stimulate imagination.

What to do In groups of 5, children make up stories – with the teacher's facilitation if necessary – on the theme of kindness. They then mime the stories. If their story demands sets or props, encourage them to use classroom objects such as rulers, bags, chairs and waste bins.

Open Forum

The teacher asks the children what they have learnt about the importance of kindness through the games in this section. Does any child need kindness to help him with a problem?

Activity 3 – Round: Kind deed

Aim To end on a positive note.

What to do Each child in turn makes a positive statement of something kind he intends to do that day, for example, 'I will help Mum with the washing up after tea', 'I will let Leroy join in our football game after lunch.'

Activity 4 – Send a ripple

Aim Ending game.

What to do The children sit in an inward-facing circle. The teacher wriggles her ten fingers, explaining she is making rain, and passes this to the child next to her. That child passes it on to the next, and so on around the circle. When all the children are wriggling their fingers, the teacher changes the action to thunder – slapping her knees – or wind – waving her arms. The teacher sends various movements around the circle in quick succession and ends by bringing out the sun – hands mime a circle.

FURTHER CLASSROOM ACTIVITIES

The Kindness Tree

Using either real twigs or a drawing of a tree, the teacher prepares cut-out leaves on which each child writes something kind that he has done. The leaves are then attached to the tree.

Booster Poster

Each child has a large sheet of paper on which he sticks a photograph of himself. Each also has five large, coloured stars. For each person five other children are invited to write kind comments on the stars, which are then stuck on the poster. The teacher should reinforce the idea of kindness before this activity to ensure that the less popular children will obtain five kind comments.

Be Kind to ... Day

The teacher puts all the children's names into a container and takes one out each day. All the children have to be kind to the named child throughout that day.

Section 5 – Friendship

Underlying moral value

The activities in this section focus on the qualities and values of friendship. The children are encouraged to explore ideals such as trust, caring and sharing. They are also confronted with the idea that whilst everyone is different, all people are worthwhile; and accepting, tolerating and celebrating people's unique differences can help create a better society.

CIRCLE MEETING 1

Activity 1 – Arm link

Aim   Fun, warm-up exercise linking arms in a symbolic gesture of friendliness.

What to do   The children form a large inward-facing circle. The teacher says the number '4'. The children have to link arms in groups of 4 around the circle, if necessary moving within the circle until they have found a group. If one or two are left they can join a group of their choice; if three children are left they can join together. When the groups are ready, the teacher tells them to cross the circle to the other side as a group. This can be repeated with groups of 5 or 6.

Activity 2 – Round: 'I like to have friends because ...'

Aim   To introduce the theme of friendship.

What to do   The children sit in an inward-facing circle. Using the conch, the children are asked in turn to complete the sentence, 'I like to have friends because ...'. They cannot use names, so no-one feels left out. Encourage them to think of statements rather than simple words like 'they are nice'. For example, 'I like to have friends because they play skipping with me at lunchtime', 'I like to have friends because they let me use their pens.'

Open Forum

The teacher asks the children what sort of things friends should do and share with each other. Examples are share hobbies and interests, care about each other, trust each other, help each other.

Does any child need help with making more friends? If so, other children should offer help, on the 'If you ...' or 'Would it help ...' model.

Activity 3 – Blindfold game

Aim   To focus on trusting someone.

What to do   The teacher tells the children that one of the things involved in friendship is trust and they are now going to play a game based on trust. The children set up an obstacle course using chairs, bags, tables and so on.

They then form pairs, each with someone they don't usually play with. One child in each pair is blindfolded. The pairs take turns to cross the obstacle course with the sighted child leading the blindfolded one and guiding her around the obstacles. When all the pairs have completed the course the children swap roles and repeat the process.

Activity 4 – Chinese mimes

Aim Ending exercise, fun.

What to do The children stand sideways in a circle, their right shoulders pointing to the centre, with their eyes closed. The teacher taps child A (the child in front of her) on the back. Child A opens her eyes and turns to face the teacher, who mimes an action. Child A turns to B (in front of her) and taps him on the shoulder. Child B opens his eyes and turns to face Child A, who repeats the teacher's mime. This continues around the circle. Once the children have completed the mime they keep their eyes open. When the mime reaches the teacher she repeats the original mime to the class to show how much it has changed.

CIRCLE MEETING 2

Activity 1 – We are all different and that's OK

Aim To help children start to think about and appreciate the differences between people.

What to do Each child is given a piece of white card. They sit in an inward-facing circle while two selected children take an ink or paint pad around. Every child presses her thumb onto the coloured pad and makes a print on the white card. The children then pass the prints round to see that every one is different and unique.

Activity 2 – Round: 'I like ...'

Aim As above.

What to do Each child in turn finishes the sentence, 'I like ...'. This can include favourite food, hobbies or clothes, but not people. The other children can say 'Yes' if they also like the same thing, but they are not allowed to say 'No' or 'Yuk' or even use any negative body language.

Open Forum

The teacher asks the children to think of other ways in which they are different – for example, body differences, hobbies, clothes, food preferences. The teacher then asks in what ways people are similar – for example, we all need food, we all need to sleep. Encourage the children to reach the idea of similar emotional needs – we all need to be liked, cared for, approved of and so on. Does anyone want some support, either for herself because she feels different, or so she can try to be kinder to someone else who is different?

Activity 3 – Mirrors

Aim   To work with someone who is not a close friend, fun ending exercise.

What to do   The children are split into pairs (A and B) and face each other. B is the mirror and has to copy all A's gestures. Tell the As to begin very slowly until the Bs have become competent. The pairs then reverse roles, so that the As become the mirrors.

CIRCLE MEETING 3

Activity 1 – Tangles

Aim   Warming-up game, to establish a feeling of co-operation.

What to do   The children stand in an inward-facing circle. They close their eyes (or use scarves as blindfolds) and slowly move towards the centre with arms outstretched. The object is for all to join hands without seeing whom they are connecting with. When this is done the children open their eyes. They must now try to untangle themselves so that they can form a circle without letting go of each other.

Activity 2 – All change

Aim   To mix the children up, fun.

What to do   The children sit in an inward-facing circle. The teacher or child calls out different categories (these could be on cards) and all the children who fit into that category have to change seats. Examples of categories: anyone with black hair, anyone with a birthday in December, anyone with a hamster.

Activity 3 – Meet my friend

Aim To establish a friendly approach to children they would not normally mix with.

What to do The children sit in an inward-facing circle. The teacher calls children alternately A and B around the circle. Each A pairs with the B on her right. The pairs are then given a set time to discover as much about each other as possible, such as likes, dislikes, hobbies and aptitudes. At the end of this time each member of the pair introduces the other to the rest with the statement, 'I'd like you to meet my friend ...' followed by three statements about the friend. For example, 'I'd like you to meet my friend Amy. She likes roast chicken. She goes to ballet lessons. Her favourite pop group is East 17.'

Open Forum

The teacher asks the children's views on the statement, 'We can't all be best friends, but it's good if we can be friendly to everyone.' They explore the idea of friendship and being friendly, why it is sometimes difficult, what sort of obstacles get in the way of friendship, why friendships are broken, what happens then and so on. Is there any child who would like help with being more friendly to others?

Activity 4 – Clapping game 2

Aim Fun, ending exercise.

What to do See page 112.

CIRCLE MEETING 4

Activity 1 – Oranges and lemons

Aim To mix up children.

What to do See page 104.

Activity 2 – Charades

Aim To discover what you have in common with others.

What to do The children form groups of 4. The teacher should try to ensure that usual bondings are separated. The children are told to discover something that the whole group likes. Ask them to try to find something a little unusual – not football or a favourite TV programme. The groups then practise miming their 'likes'. Eventually each group performs its mime to the others, who have to guess what the 'like' is. The group performing can tell the others whether it's a book, TV programme or hobby and so on.

Activity 3 – Round: 'I felt lonely when ...'

Aim To focus the children's thoughts on what it is like to be lonely.

What to do The children sit in an inward-facing circle. Using the conch each child in turn completes the sentence, 'I felt lonely when ...'. They may name an occasion in or out of school.

Open Forum

Continuing the theme of loneliness, the teacher asks what it was like to feel lonely. The children are then invited to explore the feelings of someone who has no friends, and are encouraged to show kindness and consideration to lonely children in the future. Would any child like help because she is lonely?

Activity 4 – Five pins

Aim Wind-down game.

What to do See page 120.

Activity 5 – Thank you

Aim   To reinforce the pleasure we get from friendly children.

What to do   Ask if any child would like to say, 'Thank you' to someone (not her best friend) who helped her when she was lonely. The children are encouraged to look across at the person and say her name; for example, 'Alima, I would like to thank you for including me in football.' Alima is then encouraged to say, 'Thank you, Henry.'

FURTHER CLASSROOM ACTIVITIES

Friend Picture

The children each draw a picture of their ideal imaginary friend (not anyone in the class), and write down all the things that they would like this friend to offer.

Play

Either in groups or as a class, the children make up a play about a new girl or boy in their class who has no friends and is feeling lonely. Encourage the children to consider all the different aspects of forming friendships – for example, the child is shy and does not easily respond to the other children, a child becomes jealous because her friend is spending time with the newcomer. One child decides she does not like the new child and tries to influence others to isolate the child, or the newcomer tries to gain friends by one-upmanship but alienates other children. Encourage the children to explore different situations and think of ways in which they could resolve any problems which arise.

Birthday Card

Ask each child to design and make a birthday card for a friend (anyone in or out of school). On the inside she is to write: 'You are my friend because ...'.

Advertise Yourself

Make a large advertisement powerfully telling everyone what you offer as a friend.

Section 6 – Co-operation

The games and activities in this section have been chosen to help the children learn the skills needed to co-operate with others. The activities will enhance their social skills and reinforce group identity. Children explore the idea of working democratically and solving problems together.

Underlying moral value

Be co-operative and help one another.

CIRCLE MEETING 1

Activity 1 – Arm link

Aim Fun, to introduce the theme of co-operation.

What to do See page 136.

Activity 2 – Tangles

Aim To extend the theme of co-operation.

What to do See page 138.

Open Forum

The children sit in an inward-facing circle. The teacher asks the children what things were important in making the two previous games successful. The teacher may prompt the children to discuss the importance of being helpful and working together. Does any child find it difficult to work with others, and would he like some help with this?

Activity 3 – Factories

Aim To encourage the idea of working together.

What to do The children are divided into groups of 4 or 5. The teacher explains that they work in a factory on a production line. Each group must decide on a product and every member of the group must have a task in the making of this product, each of which must be mimed. The children have an allotted time in which to decide on their product and practise their mimes. The groups then take turns to perform their pieces, during which each group member gives a commentary on his mime. The audience is told at the start of each piece what the end product is, for example: 'Our factory makes armchairs.' The sequence is as follows:

Child 1: I am making the wooden frame. *Mimes sawing, nailing together.*

Child 2: I am making the padding and cushions. *Mimes cutting foam cushions and fitting padding to chairs.*

Child 3: I am cutting out and sewing the fabric to cover the armchair. *Mimes cutting out fabric and sewing pieces together.*

Child 4:   I am fitting the covers onto the chair and cushions.
Mimes this task.
Together: Here is our finished chair.

Activity 3 – Variation

It is a good idea to ask children who are not very confident speakers to mime certain pieces of machinery. Their task in the production line is to repeat some gesture; they may even make an appropriate machine-like sound to accompany their movements. They must make sure that their movement links to the next person's mime.

Activity 4 – Send a ripple

Aim   Ending game.

What to do   See page 132.

CIRCLE MEETING 2

Activity 1 – Share a lap

Aim   To reintroduce the theme of co-operation.

What to do   The children stand in a circle, then make a quarter turn so that each child faces the back of the child in front. Make the circle move inwards, then ask each child to grasp the waist of the child in front. All try to sit on the lap of the child behind until all children are seated on a lap. The group can have several goes until this is achieved. If the children find this difficult, ask them what would be helpful – for example, silence, sitting one at a time.

Activity 2 – Share a chair

Aim   To encourage co-operation.

What to do   In pairs, the children have to devise as many different ways as possible of both occupying one chair with their feet off the ground. If you have the time, you can ask the pairs to select three of their most inventive positions and then choreograph them so that they move fluidly from one movement to the next. It would be a good idea to play a gentle piece of music to accompany these dance-like movements.

Open Forum

The children sit in an inward-facing circle. The teacher asks why it is better, if people are working together, for everyone to be co-operative. How do they know if someone isn't? What sort of problems arise if people do not co-operate? Does anyone find it hard to work with others?

Activity 3 – Problem solving

Aim To encourage co-operation.

What to do The children are divided into groups of 4. Each group is given a prepared story problem, which they have to solve with every member of the group playing a part. The following are suggested stories.

You are out playing together. Someone has left the gate of a field open and sheep are straying onto a winding country road. What could you do? (Possible solutions: try to herd sheep back into field; run in opposite directions and flag down drivers to warn them of sheep on the road; run to the nearest house to get help.)

You are out hiking in an unknown area. One member of the group falls down a cliff and is injured.

You are on holiday at the seaside. You are walking along a beach when you hear someone crying for help. You see another child stranded on a rock by the incoming tide.

Activity 4 – Wink murder

Aim Fun, ending game.

What to do The children sit in an inward-facing circle. A detective is chosen and leaves the room. A murderer is then chosen. The detective returns to stand in the centre of the circle. The murderer then winks at a chosen victim, trying to do so unobserved by the detective (winking when the detective's back is turned). The victim must die (collapse on the floor) with a shriek. The game continues with more victims until the detective identifies the murderer.

CIRCLE MEETING 3

Activity 1 – Hunt the pair

Aim   Fun, co-operation; a warming-up, mixing-up game.

What to do   The teacher prepares pictures of pairs such as bucket and spade, salt and pepper, dustpan and brush. One item is needed for each child. The pictures are put into a container and mixed up. Each child takes a picture out. When everyone has done this, the children try to find the other half of their pair in silence.

Activity 2 – Balancing your partner

Aim   Fun, co-operation.

What to do   The children may remain in their pairs from the previous round (unless this would cause problems). The pairs sit back to back with their legs outstretched and link their arms at the elbows. They try to stand, helping each other. They then sit facing with their legs outstretched, feet touching and holding hands, and try to pull each other up to a standing position.

Activity 3 – Body building

Aim   Co-operation, fun.

What to do   In groups of 4, the children are given structures to build together with their bodies – all members of the group join together to form one structure such as a bridge, a tree or a windmill.

Activity 4 – Obstacle course

Aim   Co-operation, to stimulate imagination.

What to do   In the same groups of 4, the children devise an obstacle course using whatever props they can find – for example, chairs, bags, coats, books – and making it as interesting as possible. Afterwards, each group demonstrates to the others how to use their obstacle course. The groups then take turns on each other's courses. (The teacher can bring in some other props if necessary to make things more interesting.)

Open Forum

What gets in the way of your being co-operative – thinking of things faster than someone else, being irritated by someone else, being fed-up?

Activity 5 – Round: 'I was co-operative ...'

Aim Ending activity.

What to do The children sit in an inward-facing circle. Using the conch, the children in turn finish the sentence, 'I was co-operative when ...', naming an occasion or act.

CIRCLE MEETING 4

Activity 1 – Musical islands

Aim Warming-up game, co-operation.

What to do Push back the chairs to make a larger-than-usual circle. Place sheets of newspaper on the floor, as islands. When music is played the children walk about; when it stops they must occupy an island (no feet in the water). The islands are gradually removed so that more and more children must occupy the same island and must help each other to stay on the newspaper. The game stops when it becomes obvious that all the children cannot fit onto the remaining islands.

Activity 2 – Touch down

Aim Fun, concentration, co-operation.

What to do The children form pairs. The teacher explains that when she calls a number, each pair must touch the floor with that number of points between them. They can use feet, hands, knees, elbows and heads. For example, if '3' is called, one child could stand on two feet, the other on one. If the teacher calls '1', one child must stand on one foot holding the other off the floor. This may also be done with groups of 3 or 4 to increase the fun and co-operation as children work out who must touch the floor and with what.

Activity 3 – Occupations

Aim   Co-operation.

What to do   The children form mixed groups of 4, with boys and girls in each group and preferably not with friends. They are told to find a corner to work in, quietly choosing an occupation they all like. They then practise miming the occupation of their choice. Groups can then mime their occupation to the other children, who have to guess what they are – for example, firemen, medical staff, actors.

Open Forum

The children sit in an inward-facing circle. The teacher asks if the occupation their group chose was each member's first choice. Since the groups were mixed, this was probably not the case. The teacher can then prompt the children into discussing democratic choice and the need, at times, to compromise in order to co-operate for the good of the group. Does any child need help in learning to co-operate?

Activity 4 – Musical statues with mime

Aim   Fun, ending activity.

What to do   See page 129.

CIRCLE MEETING 5

Activity 1 – Story titbits

Aim   To mix up children into groups.

What to do   The teacher prepares simple written or drawn stories which are cut into four or five sections, so that there is a section for each child. The sections are put into a container and mixed up. The teacher invites each child to take one section from the container. The children are told how many sections form the complete story. In silence they approach each other and find the missing parts to their story. They then put the story in order.

Activity 2 – Miming tasks

Aim   Co-operation.

What to do   The children remain in their groups from the previous game. Each group is given a written card with a task which they must perform in mime, with all group members taking a part. Examples are putting up a tent; collecting sticks and building a fire; digging up potatoes, washing, peeling and cooking them. When the groups have rehearsed their tasks, they show them to the others, who have to guess what they are doing.

Open Forum

The teacher prompts the children to remind themselves of what they have learnt about co-operation – that is, they need to listen, watch, be helpful, compromise, share and so on. The teacher asks for examples of how they could all be more co-operative in the classroom. How could they persuade someone to be co-operative if he wasn't – what sort of punishments or incentives could they use? Does any child need help in being more co-operative during work time in the classroom?

Activity 3 – Round: 'I'm going to be more co-operative by ...'

Aim   To establish positive aims for the future.

What to do   Using the conch, each child completes the sentence, 'I'm going to be more co-operative by ...', stating an action or behaviour he intends to adopt.

Activity 4 – Chinese mimes

Aim   Fun, ending game.

What to do   See page 137.

FURTHER CLASSROOM ACTIVITIES

Group Flags

The children are divided into groups of 4. Each group is given a large sheet of white card and four differently coloured sheets, and also four different templates such as squares, stars, triangles and circles. The children must decide who is going to cut which shape out of which colour paper. They must cut four of their shape, one in each colour. They then design a pattern on the white card, using the coloured shapes, and stick them on. The groups may also think of a motto and write it on their flags; for example: 'We all help one another', 'It's good to share.' All the flags may be displayed on the wall.

Inventions

The children are divided into groups of 4 and given an invention to devise. For example, invent a machine that makes a sandwich, taking two slices of bread, buttering them, putting a filling in, putting bread together and cutting it in half. The children draw their inventions or make one from toilet roll holders, straws, string, boxes and so on. Obviously, it does not need to work but the children must explain how their machine should operate.

Section 7 – Solving problems

The activities in this section provide the children with the opportunity to recognise when a problem exists, to study the cause and effect of problems and to find workable solutions to problems.

Underlying moral value

We all have problems at various times and sometimes we need to help people sort them out.

CIRCLE MEETING 1

Activity 1 – Zoom and eek

Aim Fun, warming-up exercise.

What to do The children sit in an inward-facing circle. One child starts a car travelling around the circle by saying 'Zoom' to the child on her right and looking him in the eyes; that child turns his head to the next player, says 'Zoom' and looks into her eyes. This action is repeated around the circle until someone says 'Eek'. The player who says 'Eek' remains facing the previous player and continues to look into her eyes to stop the action continuing further around the circle. The car then changes direction with 'Zooms' until someone else says 'Eek' and the direction changes again. See how fast the children can make the car travel and change direction.

Activity 2 – Skin the snake

Aim Fun, to introduce the theme of problem-solving.

What to do The children stand in a line one behind another and put their right hands through their legs to clasp the left hand of the player behind. The last child crouches down and tucks her head in. The other children move slowly backwards over the last child until she is at the front. The process is then repeated.

Open Forum

Ask the children if they found this game easy. What sort of difficulties did they encounter – losing balance, moving too quickly, being knocked over by someone else? Ask if they gradually became better at the game and why – moved more slowly, took more care? Can they think of another word for 'difficulty' (i.e. 'problem')? Ask them to give examples of problems. Note that since resolving conflicts and bullying are discussed in later sections, it would be better to deal with these subjects fully then. Does any child have a problem now that she needs help with?

Activity 3 – Round: 'A problem I had ...'

Aim To show that problems can be solved.

What to do Using the conch, the children tell others about a problem that they have had and how they resolved it.

Activity 4 – Pass a smile

Aim Ending game.

What to do See page 105.

CIRCLE MEETING 2

Activity 1 – Duck, duck, goose

Aim Fun, warming-up exercise.

What to do The children stand in an inward-facing circle. One child is chosen to walk around the outside of the circle. She taps each player on the shoulder, usually saying 'duck'. When the child taps a player gently on the shoulder and says 'goose', both children run around the outside of the circle in opposite directions in order to try to reach the vacant space first. The child who is last becomes 'it' and the game continues.

Activity 2 – Something is wrong

Aim To introduce the causes and effects of problems.

What to do The children form groups of 4. The teacher gives each group a simple jigsaw to put together. However, in each case, one piece of the jigsaw has been swapped with a piece from another group's puzzle. After a few minutes the teacher asks how they are getting on. When it is clear to the children that they cannot complete their puzzles, the teacher asks what is wrong. Once all the groups realise what the problem is, the teacher asks each group to hold up the piece that does not fit so that the other groups can find their missing piece and complete their jigsaws.

Open Forum

The children sit in an inward-facing circle. The teacher introduces problems to the group, who discuss the effect that the problem will have. (Examples: children are playing a game; one child has got the rules wrong. A supply teacher comes in on a lesson where the children are in groups practising plays; the teacher thinks they are messing around. A child is sent to the shops to buy some apples, but goes into the newsagents' instead.) Does any child have a problem or worry that she needs help with?

Activity 3 – Stop, think and go

Aim   To help with problem-solving.

What to do   The teacher introduces the idea of brainstorming to find possible solutions to a problem. An example is used to give unworkable solutions as well as sensible ones so that the children can see that solutions have to be realistic. For example:

> Amy is babysitting her younger sister one morning. The sister is bored. What can Amy do? The teacher asks for possible solutions (e.g., put on a video, help the sister make a card, tie the sister up, play with the sister and her toys, put the sister to bed, play dressing up, do some jigsaw puzzles, lock the sister in the garden shed).

The teacher can then ask the children to brainstorm ideas for given situations and discuss which are practical and realistic (e.g. a foreign child can only spend one day in this country and wants to learn as much as possible about typical English life; what could the children do to show this?).

Activity 4 – Electric squeeze

Aim   Ending game.

What to do   See page 129.

CIRCLE MEETING 3

Activity 1 – I know your name

Aim Fun, warming-up exercise.

What to do See page 106.

Activity 2 – Can I help?

Aim To encourage children to identify any problems they would like help with and to help the class members to understand that they are responsible for sorting out their own problems.

What to do The children sit in an inward-facing circle. They use the conch to speak. Any child can identify a problem she has by saying, 'I need help because ...'. She must not directly name another child in a negative way. Other children can offer possible solutions by asking, 'Would it help if ...?'. The child with the problem considers each solution and responds accordingly; for example: 'No, I don't think that would help me', 'Yes, that would/might help me.'

Open Forum

The teacher asks the children what sort of problems might exist in the classroom which would prevent someone from working properly; for example, a child doesn't know what to do, it's too noisy, a child does not have the correct equipment, a child has difficulty concentrating. How can these problems be resolved? Perhaps the teacher and the children will decide that a short weekly meeting would be a useful way to solve any general class problems. Perhaps a procedure could also be agreed on for individual problems to be resolved quickly and effectively. Does any child have a problem now with working in the classroom that she would like help with?

Activity 3 – Group work

Aim To help children find solutions together.

What to do The children are split into groups of 4. Each child is given a problem which the other three children in the group must try to help her resolve. For example:

Child 1:   You have to meet someone at the station. You don't know what this person looks like.

Child 2:   You are given some homework. You know nothing about the subject.

Child 3:   You want to make your mother a birthday cake, but have never cooked anything before.

Child 4:   You are invited to a cousin's party but don't know what sort of clothes you should wear.

Activity 4 – Word game

Aim   Ending game.

What to do   See page 122.

FURTHER CLASSROOM ACTIVITIES

Picture Stories

The children form groups of 4. They make up a story which they draw as a sequence of pictures in boxes. (Explain to the children that the drawings must be very explicit to show exactly what is happening.) If their drawing skills are not very good they can use stick figures or cartoons. They number the first and last box only. The pictures are cut into their separate boxes and muddled up. The groups then take turns to put each other's pictures into the correct sequence and decide what the story is.

Section 8 – Resolving conflict

The activities in this section focus the children's attention on the causes of conflict, how conflict can be resolved either between individuals or collectively as a group, and the need for children to take responsibility for their actions.

Underlying moral value

Think about other people's points of view.

CIRCLE MEETING 1

Activity 1 – Leaves, rabbits and foxes

Aim Fun, warming-up game.

What to do Push the chairs back to make a larger-than-usual circle. The children are divided into three equal-sized groups of leaves, rabbits and foxes. The foxes stand in a circle. The leaves stand anywhere inside this circle and the rabbits stand anywhere outside. On the command 'Go', the rabbits have to try to dodge past the foxes to capture a leaf, and the foxes must try to catch a rabbit. The leaves cannot move. After several minutes the game stops and everyone looks at who has been successful. The groups then swap roles and play again.

Activity 2 – Everybody's different

Aim To remind the children that everybody is unique and different from everybody else.

What to do The children sit in an inward-facing circle. The teacher calls out different categories. All the children who are included in any particular category stand. Examples are all children with brown eyes, all children who had toast for breakfast, all children who ride horses, all children who watch *Neighbours*, all children who are vegetarian.

Open Forum

Through questions and prompting the teacher leads the children to acknowledge that everyone is different. Although they might share some things in common, no two people are exactly the same. The teacher shows the children a picture of two dogs tied together. Dog A wants the bowl of dog food whilst Dog B wants the bone. They are both pulling in opposite directions and getting nowhere. The teacher asks the children what is happening, and how the situation could be resolved (e.g., A and B could both go to the bone, B picks up the bone and then both to the bowl of dog food. A could eat the dog food while B eats the bone.). Is any child involved in a conflict with someone else that she needs help with?

Activity 3 – Pairs

Aim   To practise resolving conflicts.

What to do   The children form pairs. The teacher gives each pair a card which has a conflicting situation on it. The children must think of ways to resolve the conflict. For example:

> A wants to watch a cartoon on television. B wants to watch a game show. They are both on at the same time.
> A and B both want the same reading book.
> At the funfair A wants B to go on the roller coaster; A won't go on the ride alone. B does not like the ride and doesn't want to go on.

Activity 4 – Chinese whispers

Aim   Fun to end on, co-operative game.

What to do   See page 112.

CIRCLE MEETING 2

Activity 1 – Dracula

Aim   Fun, warming-up exercise.

What to do   The children sit in an inward-facing circle. One child is chosen to be Dracula and stands in the centre. Dracula points to and names a seated child and walks in his direction. The victim must point to and name another child who is then touched by Dracula. Dracula then sets off to touch the new victim. The game continues until Dracula touches a victim before she names another child. The victim then becomes the new Dracula.

Activity 2 – Someone else's shoes

Aim   To understand someone else's point of view.

What to do   The children form pairs. They find something that one likes and the other dislikes. They then swap roles and try to think of all the reasons why they have different views, trying to feel as their partner would.

For example:

A likes *Neighbours*; B hates *Neighbours*. They swap roles.

A: I hate *Neighbours* because it's boring, the plots are really far fetched and the characters unreal. They are always discovering long-lost relatives and squabbling. Real neighbours aren't like that (etc.).

B: I like *Neighbours* because it's exciting. You get to really like or hate the characters. I'm always keen to see what's going to happen next. It's always full of surprises. I get really sad when someone leaves because I miss them. I like to talk to all my friends about *Neighbours* and we try to guess what's going to happen (etc.).

Open Forum

The teacher asks the children to think of all the reasons why people disagree (e.g., different points of view, different likes and dislikes, stubbornness, unkindness, some children are more adventurous or outgoing than others, selfishness). The teacher asks the children how they feel when they are in conflict with someone else (e.g., angry, hurt, tearful, vengeful, unhappy). Is any child unhappy because he is involved in a conflict and needs help to resolve it?

Activity 3 – Arbitration

Aim   To show the children that conflicts can be resolved.

What to do   The teacher asks the children what the best way is to deal with conflict (i.e., find a solution). The teacher then asks the children to give examples or instances of situations where they conflicted with someone. They must not name another child in a negative fashion. The other children can put forward possible solutions until an acceptable one is found.

Activity 4 – Word game

Aim   Ending exercise, fun.

What to do   See page 122.

CIRCLE MEETING 3

Activity 1 – Zoom and eek

Aim Fun, warming-up exercise.

What to do See page 154.

Activity 2 – Share a chair

Aim To generate a feeling of co-operation.

What to do See page 145.

Open Forum

The teacher asks the children how they feel when they are getting on well with one another (e.g., good, warm, happy). How does this differ from how they feel when they are in conflict with someone (e.g., angry, sad, hurt)? The teacher asks what unpleasant consequences may come from conflict (e.g., breaking friendships, fights, getting other people to gang up on someone, trying to get revenge). She asks them, 'Wouldn't it be better for everyone if conflicts could be resolved?' They then consider possible ways of resolving conflicts. For example:

Stage 1
Listen carefully to each other's point of view. Try to come to an agreement or compromise which you are both happy with. If this does not work:

Stage 2
Ask a mutually agreed third person to arbitrate. If this does not work:

Stage 3
Bring the conflict to a class circle session. All the children put forward possible solutions until an acceptable one is found. If one child is being intractable and not really looking for a solution he may need encouragement to consider his behaviour and think about why co-operation is desirable.

The teacher and children might decide on a procedure to deal with unresolved conflicts, such as holding regular circle sessions to address any conflicts, or a child asking the teacher to hold a circle session to deal with a conflict. Does any child need help with an unresolved conflict now?

Activity 3 – Round: 'I will try to ...'

Aim To encourage the children to take responsibility for their own behaviour.

What to do The teacher asks the children to think of any particular situation or behaviour which usually triggers an aggressive response from them and results in conflict. They are asked to think of a way to avoid the conflict, which they will try to carry out. The children use the conch to speak. For example: 'I will try to be kinder to my sister and let her share my computer', 'I will try to stay calm if I am not asked to play football at lunchtime.'

Activity 4 – Sausages

Aim Fun, ending game.

What to do The children sit in an inward-facing circle. One person stands in the centre and asks one child a question. The children can only respond with the word 'sausages'. For example:

Q: What do you wear on your feet?
A: *Sausages.*

Q: What's your favourite pop group?
A: *Sausages.*

Q: What do you brush your teeth with?
A: *Sausages.*

The reply must be given with a straight face; if a child smiles or laughs when answering, he takes the place of the questioner in the centre.

FURTHER CLASSROOM ACTIVITIES

Surveys

To reinforce the concept that everyone is different, the children conduct surveys in the classroom. Examples are shoe size, what everyone eats for breakfast, and what their hobbies are. The children make charts to display their results, colouring in blocks to represent children, using stick-on stars or circles or any other appropriate method.

Collage

Each child makes a collage of his favourite things. He can cut pictures out of magazines and use his own drawings and photographs or other materials.

Calm or Cross

The children make a large classroom display by choosing 'calm' or 'cross' words to put into different-coloured backgrounds. Red paper could represent 'cross' and green paper 'calm'. For example:

Calm	Cross
patient	angry
co-operative	bad-tempered
happy	unkind

Punch and Judy

In groups of 3, children make stick puppets of Punch, Judy and a third character of their own invention (e.g., Mr Sort-it-out). The children write plays in which Punch and Judy squabble until Mr Sort-it-out comes along. He sorts out the arguments and persuades Punch and Judy to be kinder and more helpful to each other. Punch and Judy then start to co-operate. The children make a stage from a cardboard box and perform their plays.

Conflict Diaries

The children are each given a prepared diary page as shown below on which they record any conflicts they are involved in over the period of one week. The teacher holds a circle session at the end of the time using the diaries as a basis for discussion about conflict resolution.

	What was the conflict about?	Who was involved?	How did you feel?	How was the conflict resolved?
Monday				
Tuesday				

Conflict Contract

In situations where conflicts have been long-standing or difficult to resolve, the teacher can add more weight to the children's solutions by producing a contract which is written up and agreed on by all parties concerned. The teacher could have pre-prepared cards as illustrated.

Name ....

I need others to ....

....

I need others not to ....

....

I will try to ....

....

Signed ....

Conflict Mediators

Children are asked to volunteer to be conflict mediators for the playground. They will each have a clip-board and paper to signify their role. Any children in dispute or annoyed with another's behaviour may consult the mediator, whose job it is to help resolve the problem without being bossy or 'preaching'. Children report back to an afternoon circle ritual on the success of this system.

Section 9 – Achieving

The activities in this section focus the children's attention on personal achievement and attaining goals. The children are shown how obstacles can affect their progress and eventual success, but that obstacles can be dealt with effectively either by personal or group effort.

Underlying moral value

We each have special strengths which we should try to make the most of.

CIRCLE MEETING 1

Activity 1 – Rainbow

Aim   Fun, warming-up game.

What to do   The children stand in an inward-facing circle. They are given the colours red, yellow, green and blue in turn. An object is placed in the centre of the circle, for example a book. The teacher calls out any of the four colours and all the children in that category run in a clockwise direction around the outside of the circle. When they reach their places again, they may enter the circle to pick up the object in the centre. Whoever picks up the object calls the next colour. To add fun, 'Rainbow' can be called while the children are running round, in which case they have to change direction and run round the circle anti-clockwise.

Activity 2 – Capture the treasure

Aim   To introduce the theme of achieving.

What to do   The children sit in an inward-facing circle. A chair is put in the centre for the keeper to sit on, and treasure (some item such as a bunch of keys) is placed under the chair. Obstacles are scattered around the circle; these could be upturned chairs, bags, scrunched-up newspaper, boxes and so on. A child is chosen to be the keeper and is blindfolded. A second child is chosen to try and capture the treasure. She must negotiate the obstacles, pick up the keys and return to her chair without being discovered by the keeper. If the keeper hears the captor, he shouts 'Stop'. The captor must freeze. The keeper points in the direction where he thinks the captor is. The keeper is not allowed to wave his hand about, but must keep it still, pointing in one direction. It is helpful if the teacher draws an imaginary line from the keeper's pointed finger to the edge of the circle. If the line does not touch the captor, she can have another try to get the treasure. If the line is correct, another child is chosen to try and capture the treasure, and the first captor becomes the keeper.

Open Forum

The children are asked what sort of things made it difficult to capture the treasure (e.g., falling over obstacles, making a noise, dropping the keys). The teacher tells the children that often in life, obstacles can stop us achieving what we want. The children are asked to think of examples of when difficulties stopped them achieving what they worked for. (Since the following activities deal fully with aspects of work and behaviour, it might be wise to concentrate on other topics at this stage; e.g., when they first rode a bicycle, when they tried to swim, when they couldn't draw something accurately.) The children use the conch to speak. Does any child need help with achieving something?

Activity 3 – Round: 'Something I achieved was ...'

Aim   To introduce the idea of enjoying a sense of achievement.

What to do   The children think of one thing that they have achieved which made them feel really good. Using the conch in turn, they complete the sentence, 'Something I achieved was ...'.

Activity 4 – Electric squeeze

Aim   Ending game.

What to do   See page 129.

CIRCLE MEETING 2

Activity 1 – Circle: Golden River

Aim   Fun, warming-up game.

What to do   The children sit in a large inward-facing circle. One child is chosen to be the keeper, and stands in the centre. The other children chant, 'Keeper, keeper, may we cross your Golden River?' The keeper replies, 'Only if you are ...' (e.g., wearing a watch, have a D in your name, have brown eyes). Any children who fit into the chosen category stand up and swap seats. Once this has been done the other children must all try to cross the circle and change seats without being caught by the keeper. A new keeper is chosen from the captives.

Activity 2 – The giant's garden

Aim   To introduce the theme of achieving.

What to do   The children sit in a large inward-facing circle. A giant is chosen to guard a garden. Paper flowers are placed on the floor near the giant. The remaining children are numbered 1 to 5 in sequence around the circle. (This is to limit the number of children moving at the same time inside the circle.) The teacher calls a number from 1 to 5 and all the children with that number enter the circle, try to capture a flower and return to their chairs without being touched by the giant. Any child who is touched must immediately return to her chair without a flower. The game continues until all the numbers have been called.

Open Forum

The teacher asks the children how they felt if they were able to get a flower (e.g., pleased, excited, successful), and how they felt if they did not (e.g., disappointed, frustrated, unsuccessful). She asks if they feel like this about school work (happy if they have produced something good; disappointed or frustrated if not). What sort of things prevent them from achieving good results in class? Examples are too much noise, not understanding instructions, finding the work too difficult, not being able to concentrate, and not having the right equipment. The teacher asks the children what might help them achieve good work in the classroom. Examples:

> 'Do not disturb' signs. The children could each make a sign out of card which they place on their table when they want to concentrate on a task undisturbed. The teacher might like to designate a table as a special work area. Children may elect, or take turns, to sit and work at this table for a given task. This must be seen as a privilege; anyone who uses the table incorrectly, disturbing others for example, or not concentrating on the task, has to leave it. The children may like to draw up a checklist for display which they can use as a 'reminder' before beginning work, with items such as 'Do you have the books you need?', 'Do you have the correct equipment – pencil, ruler, rubber?'

If any child is having problems in achieving something, would she like help?

Activity 3 – Round: 'I am going to try harder ...'

Aim To make a positive statement to enhance achievement.

What to do Using the conch, each child makes a positive statement about one way in which she is going to try and achieve better results in her work; for example, 'I am going to try harder to listen to the teacher's instructions', 'I am going to try harder to write neatly', 'I am going to try harder to stop chatting to other people when I should be working.'

Activity 4 – Word game

Aim Ending game.

What to do See page 122.

CIRCLE MEETING 3

Activity 1 – Cat and mouse

Aim Warming-up game, fun.

What to do The children stand in an inward-facing circle holding hands. One child is chosen to be the mouse and stands inside the circle. A second child is the cat and stands outside. On the command 'Go', both children dodge in and out of the circle under the other children's arms. The cat has to try to catch the mouse.

Activity 2 – Role play

Aim To introduce the theme of taking responsibility for one's own behaviour.

What to do In groups of 4, the children are given imaginary tasks to perform, for example putting up a tent, getting out tables and chairs. Each child in the group is told to behave in a certain way and instructed to concentrate on being this all the time (e.g., sulky, bossy, lazy, bad-tempered, unkind). The children are asked to explore, through role play, what would happen if they set about their given task as a group, but behaved in their allotted manner.

Open Forum

The children sit in an inward-facing circle. The teacher asks if they actually managed to complete their imaginary tasks. Was it difficult and if so why? The teacher guides the discussion so that the children realise and acknowledge that certain aspects of their behaviour could affect their own and other people's achievement. Does any child need help because her behaviour is affecting her own and others' ability to achieve?

Activity 3 – Round: 'I think I could do better if ...'

Aim To make a positive statement to enhance achievement by taking responsibility for one's behaviour.

What to do Using the conch, the children complete the sentence, 'I could do better if ...' (e.g., 'I didn't sulk', 'I wasn't grumpy', 'I tried to be kinder').

Activity 4 – Wink murder

Aim Ending game.

What to do See page 146.

CIRCLE MEETING 4

Activity 1 – Squeak, piggy, squeak

Aim Fun, warming-up game.

What to do The children sit in an inward-facing circle. One child is chosen to be blindfolded and stand in the centre of the circle; a second child leads the blind one. The second child turns the blind one around several times so that she is disorientated, then leads her across the circle to sit on another child's lap. The blind child commands, 'Squeak, piggy, squeak.' The seated child squeaks three times and the blind child has to try and guess his identity. The game continues until the blind child makes a correct guess.

Activity 2 – Drama

Aim To explore the feeling of achievement and success.

What to do The teacher asks the children to push the chairs back and create a larger circle. She tells them they are going on a journey. They must act out what happens and try to imagine how they feel as they travel. The teacher provides them with all kinds of obstacles and difficulties to overcome. For example:

> They have to cross a sticky, muddy swamp.
> They walk through a field of prickly thistles.
> They have to climb a steep mountain.
> They come across an injured traveller whom they have to carry to a hospital.
> They have to cross a plain inhabited by hungry wolves.
> After many obstacles and difficulties they reach their destination and celebrate.

Open Forum

The children sit in an inward-facing circle. The teacher asks how they felt while they were on the journey and when they reached their destination. She asks how these feelings relate to their work in school. The children are prompted to acknowledge that success is a good feeling. The teacher asks what might help them to succeed in their work. Examples are:

> Short-term goals. Children set themselves realistic short-term (e.g., weekly) goals. They can decide on suitable rewards for achieving these.
> Each child has a special day or week during which all the other children help her to achieve a set goal, either in work or behaviour. (This can be particularly helpful for a child with persistent behaviour problems.)
> Children are given responsibility badges for a day or week and take charge of a special job in the classroom (e.g., giving out books, collecting pencils). This can either be used as a reward for achieving good behaviour or as an aid to promoting good behaviour.

Does any child need special help in order to achieve in the classroom?

Activity 3 – Round: 'Something I would like to achieve is ...'

Aim To create a positive attitude to achieving.

What to do Using the conch, the children complete the statement, 'Something I would like to achieve is ...'.

Activity 4 – Arm link

Aim Fun, ending game.

What to do See page 136.

FURTHER CLASSROOM ACTIVITIES

Congratulatory Stationery

The children design a congratulatory letter to give to another child when she has achieved something. The teacher could use congratulatory letters for a child to take home when she has made a positive effort to improve her behaviour.

Teacher's letter

> Longacre School
> Worthy
> 15 June 1995
>
> Dear Mr & Mrs Johns
>
> I am pleased to inform you that David has made a positive effort this term in his behaviour. Thank you for your support.
>
> Yours sincerely
>
> *Mary Dogood*
>
> Mrs M. Dogood

Child's letter

> Dear Wei
>
> Well done for writing such a good story
>   from
>
>   Sita

Achievement House

The teacher gives each child a piece of paper in the shape of a brick on which to note something good that she has achieved. All the bricks are used in a collage (e.g., a house) and displayed on the wall.

Achievement Ladders

Each child has a ladder for a long-term (half-term or term) goal. With the teacher's help the child decides on stages (rungs) up to the desired goal. There could be small incentives to climb each rung and an agreed reward on reaching the top. The children use a card figure or a coloured circle to 'climb' the ladder. If the ladder is for improving behaviour, the child could go down a rung for a 'bad' week. She would then have to have two good weeks before earning the next incentive. Two examples are shown.

Achievement

Write a whole story in neat handwriting.

Write a letter in neat handwriting.

Copy a poem in neat handwriting.

Write a paragraph in neat handwriting.

Write name, age and address in neat handwriting.

Copy out one sentence in neat handwriting.

Symbert's ladder

Incentive

My teacher gives me a special certificate to show I have achieved good handwriting.

Congratulatory letter to take home. I can show my work to the headteacher. My teacher will put my work up on the wall.

I can choose my favourite game in PE.

The class gives me a clap for reaching half-way.

I write the day and date on the blackboard.

I get a smiley sticker.

Achievement

I have been good for six whole weeks.

I have made a really big effort.

I have been good all week.

I am half-way, with another good week.

I have not disrupted a lesson for two weeks.

I have worked hard all week.

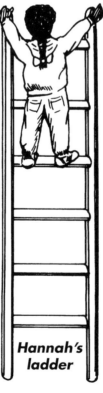

Hannah's ladder

Incentive

Congratulatory letter to take home. I can help the caretaker for a morning. The headteacher gives me a badge for good behaviour.

I can bring my favourite toy or game to school to play with at lunchtime. I can help the teacher with equipment.

I can collect and return the register to the office. I can be in charge of playground equipment for a week.

I can be first in the playground queue. I can have first choice at activities time. The class gives me a clap for trying hard.

My teacher gives me a special job to do.

I get five extra minutes of games or privilege time.

Section 10 – Changes

The activities in this section focus the children's attention on the various changes that occur in people's lives and how they can be affected by them.

Underlying moral value

Accept change as a natural part of life.

CIRCLE MEETING 1

Activity 1 – Oranges and lemons

Aim   Fun, warming-up game.

What to do   See page 104.

Activity 2 – Round: 'What I'd like to change ...'

Aim   To introduce the theme of changes.

What to do   The children stand in an inward-facing circle. They take turns to complete the sentence, 'What I'd like to change about myself is ...' (e.g., 'my hair; I'd like it to be curly', 'my height; I'd like to be taller', 'my nose; it's too big').

Activity 3 – Brainstorm

Aim   To focus on changes they have experienced.

What to do   The teacher asks the children to think of all the changes that happen or have happened to them in their lives. These can be mundane or big events (e.g., new school, moving house, new hairstyle, birth of brother or sister, new teacher, new three-piece suite).

Open Forum

The teacher asks the children whether changes are good or bad. The response will be that some are good, some bad. Why is this? The children are prompted to think of changes they have experienced and how they have been affected – have changes made them happy or miserable? Is there any child who is unhappy because of a change in his life who would like some help?

Activity 4 – Rainbow

Aim   Ending game.

What to do   See page 170.

CIRCLE MEETING 2

Activity 1 – Zoom and eek

Aim Warming-up game.

What to do See page 154.

Activity 2 – Change of identity

Aim To focus children's attention on change, fun.

What to do The children form pairs. They question each other for several minutes about likes, dislikes, hobbies, interests and so on. They then swap identities. Each child, in turn, introduces himself as the other person and says three things about that person as though he were talking about himself.

Activity 3 – Round: 'A change that made me miserable was ...'

Aim To introduce this theme for discussion.

What to do Each child in turn completes the sentence, 'A change that made me miserable was ...'. Each recalls an occasion from his life when change had an adverse effect on him. For example:

> 'when I moved house and didn't see my friends any more'
> 'when my brother was born and got all Mum's attention'
> 'when my mum and dad got divorced'
> 'when my grandad died'.

Open Forum

The teacher asks the children to think of ways of dealing with negative feelings and emotions brought on by change. The children are also given the opportunity to share similar experiences and discuss how they reacted. The teacher asks the children to think about what would help them cope with negative changes; for example, talking to a close friend, asking a trusted adult for advice, holding a circle session for advice from the group. Does any child need help with any change that is making him unhappy?

Activity 4 – Five pins

Aim　Fun, ending game.

What to do　See page 120.

CIRCLE MEETING 3

Activity 1 – All change

Aim　Fun, warming-up game.

What to do　See page 138.

Activity 2 – Faces 1

Aim　To focus children's attention on feelings.

What to do　See page 120.

Activity 3 – Changes chart

Aim　To compare and discuss how changes affected the children and to share feelings.

What to do　The children work in pairs. The teacher gives each child a prepared list of changes that he might have experienced. The children look through the list and discuss with their partners how they felt or might feel about each situation. The list should include a variety of good and bad changes; for example, growing taller, having a bad haircut, changing schools, making a new friend, having to talk in front of the class, getting a new pair of shoes.

Open Forum

To raise the children's awareness of the anxieties of changing schools and of how they can help new pupils.

The teacher has a brief discussion with the children, asking them what it would feel like to start at a new school. What could the other children do to help? For example:

give the new child a tour of inspection,
explain the rules,
tell the child about any extra-curricular activities,
introduce the child to all the teachers,
explain the privileges and sanctions used,
explain classroom procedure.

In pairs the children take turns at being the new pupil, while their partners welcome and help them settle in. Does any child have an anxiety he wishes to discuss and have help with?

Activity 4 – Round: 'I am looking forward to ...'

Aim   To anticipate and look forward to change.

What to do   Each child in turn completes the sentence, 'I am looking forward to ...', stating a change that is going to happen to him; for example, 'going on holiday with the Cubs', 'learning to dive', 'writing with an ink pen'.

FURTHER CLASSROOM ACTIVITIES

Personal History

Using photographs, drawings and memorabilia, the children make a personal history of their lives from birth to the present time, recording all the important changes that have taken place. It may help to show the following example.

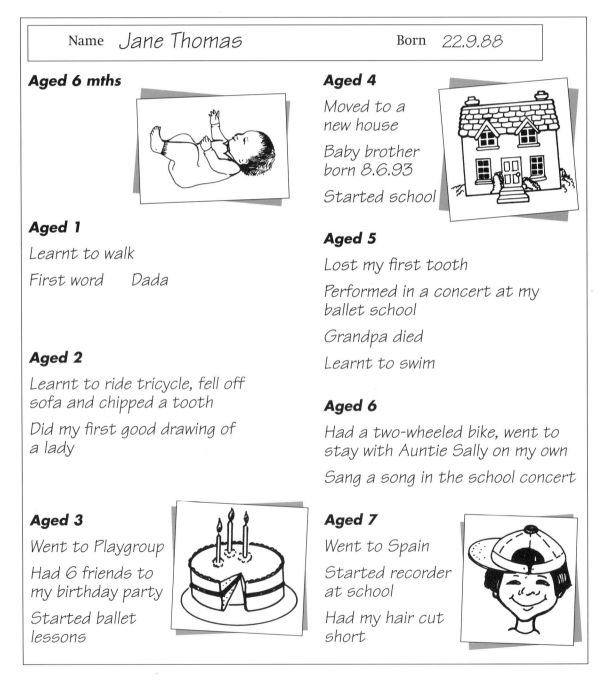

Name *Jane Thomas*   Born *22.9.88*

Aged 6 mths

Aged 1

Learnt to walk

First word   Dada

Aged 2

Learnt to ride tricycle, fell off sofa and chipped a tooth

Did my first good drawing of a lady

Aged 3

Went to Playgroup

Had 6 friends to my birthday party

Started ballet lessons

Aged 4

Moved to a new house

Baby brother born 8.6.93

Started school

Aged 5

Lost my first tooth

Performed in a concert at my ballet school

Grandpa died

Learnt to swim

Aged 6

Had a two-wheeled bike, went to stay with Auntie Sally on my own

Sang a song in the school concert

Aged 7

Went to Spain

Started recorder at school

Had my hair cut short

Seasons

The children draw or make collage pictures of the four seasons. They record the things they like and dislike about each season.

Drama

In groups of 4 the children write a play exploring their emotions about and reactions to a change. They may take on other roles (e.g., another member of their family, an adult in a workplace). The teacher could give them some ideas to work on which are age appropriate, for example:

> death of a relative,
> parents' divorce,
> being made redundant,
> having to cope while mother is hospitalised,
> their first holiday on their own.

Section 11 –
Some extra ideas

This section offers a variety of topics for discussion with ideas and activities for each theme. If it is felt that any of the topics needs further exploration or is particularly relevant to your school, the activities may be expanded and additional lessons planned around issues arising out of the initial discussion. Topics covered are:

name-calling,
physical bullying,
gender,
racism,
assertiveness.

NAME-CALLING

Activity 1 – I know your name

Aim Fun, warming-up exercise, to introduce the theme of name-calling.

What to do See page 106.

Activity 2 – Action name game

Aim Fun, to introduce the theme of name-calling.

What to do The children stand in an inward-facing circle. Each child thinks of an action adjective which begins with the same initial as his or her name, for example:

> skipping Sally,
> tunnelling Tom,
> leaping Leslie,
> crouching Catherine.

The children take turns to say their action names and all the other children mime each action.

Open Forum

The children sit in an inward-facing circle. The teacher asks if they enjoyed the name games. She asks if anyone is called a name she does not like and which upsets her. Using the conch, the children give their answers by saying, 'I do not want people to call me ...'. What sort of things do people get called names about? (Examples are appearance, weight, clothes, accent and names.) What does it feel like to be called an unpleasant name? Ask the children to give responses saying, 'I feel ...' (e.g., horrid, embarrassed, unhappy, angry). The children are asked what can be done to stop name-calling. (For example, 'Ask the offender to think how she would feel if she were called by an unpleasant name', 'Tell the teacher.' The children may each make a resolution to consider others' feelings and not call anyone by an unkind name. Other children may decide to stand by the victim and ask the offender to be kinder. Any offender could be required to stand up during class time and publicly apologise to the victim.

Activity 3 – Saying sorry

Aim To help children disentangle themselves from negative interactions and start afresh.

What to do Any child who wishes to apologise to another for regular name-calling raises a hand. She will look at her victim and say, for example, 'David, I'm sorry I called you that name!' (avoid using the unpleasant name). The victim responds by saying, 'That's all right, Fatima.' Remind the children that if they choose to do this, they must have the intention of not using the unpleasant name again. At the next circle meeting the victim may congratulate those children who have kept to their agreement and desisted from name-calling.

Activity 4 – Affirmation

Aim To end with positive statements.

What to do Each child in turn introduces herself or himself and states something she or he is good at. For example:

> 'My name is John Davies and I am good at computer games.'
> 'My name is Sarah Matthews and I am good at dancing.'
> 'My name is Jenny Thomas and I am good at drawing.'

PHYSICAL BULLYING

Activity 1 – Rainbow

Aim Warming-up game.

What to do See page 170.

Activity 2 – The giant's garden

Aim To introduce the theme of bullying.

What to do See page 172.

Open Forum

The teacher asks the children how they would feel if the giant had been real (e.g., scared, frightened). Why would they feel like this? Answers may be: 'The giant might really capture me', 'The giant might hurt me', 'The giant might eat me.' She asks the children what sort of behaviour from other children frightens them in the playground (e.g., being pushed, being kicked, being punched). She asks the children why some children bully others. Answers may be: 'They don't know how to be kind', 'They always want their own way', 'They like to be tough.' The teacher asks the children what they think of bullies, stressing that no-one is to be named. Possible answers are: 'They're horrid', 'I hate them', 'I just pretend to be their friend so they won't pick on me.' She asks if it is easy to report incidents of bullying. Answers may include: 'No, because if I tell on someone she might bash me up again', 'We don't say anything about someone hurting another child in case she picks on us instead.' She then asks the children to think of ideas which could become classroom policy that would help prevent bullying. For example:

- Any reported incidents will be treated with confidentiality. Isolated incidents of bullying will be punished with known sanctions, e.g., loss of privilege time, exclusion from favourite activity.
- Persistent bullying could be tackled by drawing up a contract with the offender, detailing the behaviour concerned and perhaps incorporating a reward for good behaviour. The class, as a group, could become involved in helping a persistent bully break a negative behaviour pattern by offering congratulations after a certain time and encouragement to stop bullying.
- Bully-box for anonymous reports of bullying.
- The children should unite against bullying and not side with a bully in order to avoid conflict.

Does any child need help because she is being bullied? Would any child like help to stop bullying other children?

Activity 3 – Clapping game 2

Aim   Fun, ending game.

What to do   See page 112.

GENDER

Activity 1 – Chinese mimes

Aim   Warming-up game

What to do   See page 137.

Activity 2 – Oranges and lemons

Aim   Fun, to introduce the theme of gender.

What to do   See page 104.

Open Forum

The teacher says that oranges and lemons are different, but they are both fruit. If girls are oranges and boys are lemons, what are they collectively (e.g., people, human beings)? She asks in which ways boys and girls are the same; possible answers are: 'They both need to eat', 'They both like friends'. She asks if girls and boys should have equal opportunities in all things. She should guide the discussion so that the children appreciate that capability should determine the opportunities a person has and the choices a person makes. Does any child have a problem because of gender that she would like help with?

Activity 3 – Round

Aim   To encourage empathy.

What to do   Each child has the opportunity to name an occasion or event when she was unable to do something she wanted to, either because of actual gender discrimination or self-imposed gender discrimination. Each could say, 'I wanted to ... but I didn't/couldn't because ...'.

Activity 4 – Gender name call

Aim   Fun, ending exercise.

What to do   The children stand in an inward-facing circle. A girl calls a boy's name and throws him a ball or beanbag, he then calls a girl's name and throws the ball or beanbag to her. The game continues with each child throwing to the opposite sex until all the children have had a turn.

RACISM

Activity 1 – Pass a smile

Aim To create a friendly feeling.

What to do See page 105.

Activity 2 – Pass the mask

Aim To introduce the theme of racism.

What to do The teacher prepares or buys a collection of masks of different ethnic groups (e.g., African, Chinese, Indian, South American, Eskimo). The children sit in an inward-facing circle. The masks are passed around for the children to try on. The teacher should try to have several mirrors so that the children can see themselves, as well as the other children, wearing the masks.

Open Forum

The teacher asks the children what they thought about their own and others' appearance when wearing the masks (e.g., funny, different). She asks what they think about people from other ethnic groups who do not look the same as them. Possible answers include: 'They're different', 'They eat funny food', 'They have funny names', 'They do different things to us.' She then asks the children in what ways they are the same. Once the children have listed the obvious physical similarities, the teacher prompts them to name emotional needs (e.g., to be accepted and liked, to have friends, to have one's views listened to and taken account of, to feel physically safe). She asks the children to try to imagine what it would be like to be in a community where they, as members of an ethnic minority, were picked on or segregated. How would they feel? Would they think it was fair behaviour? What might their reactions be?

The teacher then asks what kind of things could help prevent racism, guiding the discussion so that children consider such things as tolerance, caring, celebrating rituals and customs, values, gaining more knowledge and understanding of the different ways of living that other ethnic groups have and challenging unfounded stereotypes (e.g., all French people smell of garlic, all Africans are lazy, Irish people are stupid). Does any child have a problem because of her race/colour/name that she would like help with?

Activity 3 – Role play

Aim   To encourage empathy.

What to do   In groups of 5, the children are given a situation concerned with racism; for example, in a local shop, in the playground, in a youth club. One member of the group plays the antagonist and taunts a second member, the victim. The remaining three players have to decide and role play how they would react and what they would say.

ASSERTIVENESS

Activity 1 – Duck, duck, goose

Aim   Fun, warming-up exercise.

What to do   See page 155.

Activity 2 – Storyline

Aim   To introduce the theme of assertiveness.

What to do   The teacher tells the children two short stories in which someone is pressurised to do something she does not want to do.

Example 1
Two friends persuade a third to sneak into the classroom during the lunchtime break and hide the books their teacher has placed on the front desk ready for the afternoon's lesson. The two friends coerce the third with taunts of cowardice or threats until she gives in.

Example 2
Anissa wants Ian to play catch with her and two friends. Ian wants to play power rangers. Anissa tells Ian he is mean and she won't be his friend unless he joins in the game. Ian is worried that Anissa will stop being his friend and also get the two others to gang up on him, so he agrees.

Open Forum

The teacher asks the children if they have ever been in a situation where they felt under pressure to do something that they didn't want to do. The children must not name other children in a negative way. She asks the children why people behave like this. Possible answers are: fear of being rejected by their peers, fear of ridicule, not wanting to be different, fear of physical hurt, wanting to be liked/admired. She asks the children what might help them become more assertive. Does any child need help now to be assertive if she is in a situation she is unhappy about?

Activity 3 – Role play

Aim   To practise being assertive.

What to do   See page 173.

Section 12 –
Just for fun

This section contains fun activities suitable for end-of-term or light-hearted circle sessions.

CIRCLE MEETING 1

Activity 1 – Oranges and lemons

What to do   See page 104.

Activity 2 – I know your name

What to do   See page 106.

Activity 3 – Numbers change

What to do   The children sit in an inward-facing circle. They are numbered 1 to 5 consecutively around the circle. One child is chosen to stand in the centre and be the caller. The caller calls out any number from 1 to 5. All the children with that number stand up and swap places. The caller tries to sit in a vacant chair. The child who is left without a chair becomes the caller.

Activity 4 – Wink murder

What to do   See page 146.

CIRCLE MEETING 2

Activity 1 – Duck, duck, goose

What to do   See page 155.

Activity 2 – Pile up

What to do   The children sit in an inward-facing circle. Each child in turn gives the command that any child fitting into the category they name is to move one place to the left. Each child names a different category. Categories named can include such things as: brown hair, blue eyes, birthday in March, dog owner, having a sister. If someone is already occupying the chair to the left, the mover has to sit on his lap. If several children are occupying a chair and one of them fits into the named category, all the children on that chair move simultaneously. The game ends when the pile up can no longer be contained.

Activity 3 – Spin the plate

What to do   The children sit in an inward-facing circle. They are numbered from 1 upwards around the circle. A child is chosen to spin a plastic plate and call out a number. The child whose number has been called must try to reach the plate before it stops spinning. He then spins the plate and calls another number, and so the game continues.

Activity 4 – Skin the snake

What to do   See page 154.

CIRCLE MEETING 3

Activity 1 – Hide the ring

What to do   The children sit in an inward-facing circle. A length of string which will stretch around the circle is needed. A ring (or any other suitable object) is threaded onto the string and the two ends are tied together so that the string is joined in a continuous circle. A child is chosen to be the guesser and leaves the room. The remaining children all hold the string with both hands and pass the threaded ring from child to child along the string, attempting to conceal its whereabouts. The guesser is invited back and must try to locate the ring. Children can pretend to pass it on, to make the game more fun. A child is allowed three guesses, then someone else has a turn to be the guesser.

Activity 2 – Sausages

What to do   See page 166.

Activity 3 – Crawl forward

What to do   The children are numbered 1 or 2 alternately around the circle. They get down on their hands and knees and when the teacher calls '1' or '2' the designated children move one limb forward. The object of the game is to cross the circle to the other side. A lot of manoeuvring will be needed as children meet in the middle.

Activity 4 – Dracula

What to do See page 163.

CIRCLE MEETING 4

Activity 1 – Word game

What to do See page 122.

Activity 2 – Own goal

What to do The children stand in an outward-facing circle with their legs apart and feet touching their neighbours'. The children must bend down and look between their legs. The teacher starts a ball rolling backwards and forwards across the circle. The children must prevent the ball passing out of the circle between their legs and roll it in another direction. One child stands outside the circle to retrieve the ball. If any player allows the ball to pass out of the circle he becomes the retriever until another lets the ball out.

Activity 3 – Fishes in the sea

What to do The children stand in an inward-facing circle. They are named 'Cod', 'Haddock', 'Plaice' and 'Whiting' in turn. When a fish name is called out, the children in that category move clockwise around the outside of the circle, and then back to their places. They are instructed how to move by various commands:

> *'high tide'*: move quickly
> *'low tide'*: move slowly
> *'tide turns'*: change direction
> *'fisherman about'*: crawl on hands and knees to avoid nets
> *'sharks'*: walk backwards
> *'coral reef'*: jump.

Activity 4 – Clapping game 2

What to do See page 112.

CIRCLE MEETING 5

Activity 1 – Spider's web

What to do   See page 130.

Activity 2 – Mouse tails

What to do   Each child is given a tail – a length of string (approximately 8 inches long) which he tucks into one of his shoes. The object of the game is for each child to try, whilst moving around within the circle, to remove other children's tails by standing on them without losing his own or forcefully removing anyone's shoe.

Activity 3 – Leaves, rabbits and foxes

What to do   See page 162.

Activity 4 – Who stole the cookies?

What to do   The children sit in an inward-facing circle. They are numbered from 1 upwards. They chant and clap to a regular rhythm, as follows:

All:	Who stole the cookies from the cookie jar?
	(clap, clap, clap, clap, clap, clap, clap, clap)
All:	Number 1 stole the cookies from the cookie jar.
	(clap, clap, clap, clap, clap, clap, clap, clap, clap)
No. 1:	Who, me?
	(clap, clap)
All:	Yes, you.
	(clap, clap, clap, clap)
No. 1:	Couldn't be.
	(clap clap)
All:	Then who?
	(clap, clap, clap, clap)
No. 1:	Number X [chooses a number] stole the cookies from the cookie jar.
	(clap [appropriate number], clap, clap, clap, clap, clap, clap, clap)

The person numbered responds and continues the sequence. The sequence is repeated until everyone has had a turn.

Section 13 – Key Stage 1

For nursery, reception and infant classes, overall Circle-Time plans are shorter and simpler. Activities focus on the underlying moral values governing the Golden Rules.

> Everyone is special.
> Be kind and help each other.
> Be gentle.
> Concentrate on your task.
> Listen carefully.

CIRCLE MEETING 1

Remind the children of Circle-Time rules:

> Hands up to speak.
> Take turns to speak.
> Look at the person who is speaking.
> Listen carefully.
> Don't spoil games.

 ### Activity 1 – Pass a smile

Aim   To establish concentration.

What to do   See page 105.

Activity 2 – Talking Ted

Aim   To introduce a talking object.

What to do   The children sit in an inward-facing circle. The teacher introduces them to the talking object, in this activity a teddy bear called Talking Ted. The teacher explains that when a child holds Ted she is allowed to speak, otherwise she must be very quiet. Ted is passed around the circle. As each child holds Ted she stands up and says, 'My name is ...'. Any child may elect to pass.

Open Forum

The teacher asks the children if they enjoyed the previous activity. Does any child find it hard to speak out? What might help her? Would she like to whisper something to the teacher, who could then pretend that Talking Ted is speaking on her behalf?

Activity 3 – Simon says

Aim   Fun, ending game.

What to do   See page 114.

Development   Because very young children are used to this activity, it's a good idea to extend the potential of the game. For example, 'Simon says put your hands on your head'; 'Simon says look down on your knees and you will find some magic sweets'; 'Simon says pretend it's one of your favourite sweets and pop one into your mouth'; 'Simon says you're feeling so happy and kind that you decide to offer a sweet to the people either side of you, telling them what sort of sweet it is' (Teacher demonstrates with her neighbours: 'Would you like one of my jelly babies?' and waits for child to answer either 'Yes, please' or 'No, thank you'); 'Simon says you're feeling so brave and kind you want to take your sweets across the circle to somebody you don't normally play with'; 'Simon says put up your hand if you would like to do this' (Teacher demonstrates). When a few children have done this, one at a time, the teacher allows all the children to move around in the centre with their sweets. Then she continues: 'Simon says go back to your seats, put your sweet papers in the waste bin beside you'; 'Simon says fold your arms, we have now finished this game.' She asks the children to give one another a pat on the back, saying, 'Well done for being kind and sharing.'

CIRCLE MEETING 2

Remind the children of circle rules (see page 202).

Activity 1 – All change

Aim   Warming-up game.

What to do   See page 138.

Activity 2 – Let me introduce myself

Aim   To encourage everyone to participate in Circle Time.

What to do   See page 104. Tell the children that once they have had a turn they fold their arms and cannot be chosen again.

Open Forum

The teacher asks if the children enjoyed the game. What did they like or dislike about it?

Activity 3 – Keeping quiet

Aim To establish concentration and turn taking.

What to do The children pass round a tambourine as quietly as possible, trying not to make any sound at all.

Activity 4 – Send a ripple

Aim Fun, ending game.

What to do See page 132.

Variation For very young children, the teacher gets them to send the rain round first and sends the thunder round only if they have the ability. If they are not ready for this, she moves from the rain to the sun coming out. She explains that after the rain, the whole circle can bring the sun out together by folding their arms, breathing in through their noses and lifting their arms like the rays of the sun, then slowly letting the air out through their mouths as they lower their arms. When all the air has gone they smile at everyone in the circle as if they were great big suns.

CIRCLE MEETING 3

The teacher asks if any child can remind the rest of the circle rules (see page 202).

Activity 1 – Clap and touch

Aim Warming-up game to establish concentration.

What to do The children sit in an inward-facing circle. They are to copy the teacher's movements. The teacher gives two claps and touches a part of her body with both hands (e.g., clap clap touch head, clap clap touch knees, clap clap touch ears, clap clap touch shoulders).

Variation As their concentration skills develop, the teacher uses a different number of claps for different body parts (e.g., 1 clap – knees, 2 claps – head, 3 claps – shoulders). Then she stops demonstrating and just claps the requisite numbers to see if the children can remember how many claps there are for each body part.

Activity 2 – I am special

Aim   Personal affirmation.

What to do   Prior to the lesson, the teacher puts a mirror inside a box. She tells the children that if they look inside the box they will see someone who is special. They must keep very quiet when they have looked and not tell anyone else who the special person is. The teacher takes the box round the circle so that each child can look inside in turn. When all the children have had a turn the teacher asks who the special person was. The children reply, 'Me'.

Open Forum

The teacher asks the children why each person is special.

Activity 3 – Round: 'Something I am good at is ...'

Aim   Personal affirmation.

What to do   Using Talking Ted, each child completes the sentence, 'Something I am good at is ...'.

Activity 4 – We are special

Aim   Team building.

What to do   The teacher and children stand up and hold hands. They swing their arms as they chant, 'We are special.' On the word 'special' they all, still holding hands, raise their arms above their heads. They then lower their arms and repeat the sentence.

CIRCLE MEETING 4

Remind children of the circle rules (see page 202).

Activity 1 – Simon says

Aim   Warming-up game.

What to do   See page 114.

Activity 2 – Round: 'Something I like about myself is ...'

Aim Personal affirmation.

What to do The children sit in an inward-facing circle. Using Talking Ted, each child completes the sentence, 'Something I like about myself is ...', naming one physical feature.

Open Forum

The children say things they like about people in the class. Then, without naming anyone, they say one thing they dislike about being in their class or in the playground. Young children need constantly reminding not to say another child's name in a negative way; they do remember this eventually.

Activity 3 – Clapping game 3

Aim Fun, ending game.

What to do The teacher tells the children that one clap means stand, two claps mean march on the spot and three claps mean sit. She or a child stands in the centre and claps instructions. The children must listen very carefully to the clapped instructions each time so they follow them correctly.

CIRCLE MEETING 5

Remind the children of the circle rules (see page 202).

Activity 1 – Pass a handshake

Aim Warming-up game.

What to do This is a variation on Pass a smile; see page 105.

Activity 2 – Round: 'If I were an animal I'd like to be ...'

Aim Personal affirmation.

What to do The children sit in an inward-facing circle. Using Talking Ted, each child in turn completes the sentence: 'If I were an animal I'd like to be ...'.

Open Forum

The teacher asks why they chose their particular animal. Answers may be: 'because it climbs well', 'because it can run fast', 'because it's pretty'. The teacher asks if there is something they would like to be better at? If they had to tell someone about a special strength they have, what would it be?

Activity 3 – Marching

Aim Ending game.

What to do See page 115.

CIRCLE MEETING 6

Remind the children of the circle rules (see page 202).

Activity 1 – Pass the keys

Aim To introduce the theme of listening

What to do The children sit in an inward-facing circle. The teacher tells them that they have to pass a bunch of keys (or any other noisy object) around the circle and try not to make any sound. They must all keep very quiet while they play this game.

Activity 2 – Noises

Aim   To practise listening carefully.

What to do   The teacher has three 'noises' in a box, hidden from the children (e.g., scrunchy paper, a rattle, a hooter). Each noise is a different instruction, for example:

> Rattle: stand, hands on head.
> Scrunchy paper: kneel on all fours.
> Hooter: sit, fold arms.

The children have to keep very quiet and listen carefully to their instructions.

Open Forum

The teacher asks what helps the children to listen well (i.e., everyone being quiet). She asks what helps them hear what she is saying as well as being quiet (i.e., looking at the teacher). She then asks if any child has a problem hearing what she says, and if any child has a problem listening (e.g., they are easily distracted, do not concentrate). The teacher asks what might help the children to listen more carefully.

Activity 3 – Musical scenes

Aim   Ending exercise to practise listening.

What to do   The children sit or lie down and close their eyes. The teacher plays a selection of different music and asks the children to think what type of scene or activity the music suggests to them. The teacher asks the children what they thought of between the pieces.

CIRCLE MEETING 7

Remind the children of the circle rules (see page 202).

Activity 1 – Duck, duck, goose

Aim   Fun, warming-up game.

What to do   See page 155.

Activity 2 – Reflections

Aim   To introduce the theme of concentration.

What to do   The children stand in an inward-facing circle. The teacher tells them that they are her reflection and have to copy everything that she does. She tells the children to watch closely and think carefully about which arm/leg to use. The teacher performs simple actions (e.g., mimes brushing hair, getting dressed, hanging out the washing).

Open Forum

The teacher asks the children what they needed to do to be good reflections (i.e., watch, think, concentrate). When do the children need to concentrate in school? Does any child find it hard to concentrate? What might help?

Activity 3 – Music and movement

Aim   To practise concentration, boost self-esteem.

What to do   The children stand in an inward-facing circle. The teacher plays some 'fun' music. One child stands in the centre and performs a simple movement (e.g., raises and lowers outstretched arms) to the beat of the music. The teacher and children copy the movement. Another child is then chosen to stand in the centre and perform a new movement.

Activity 4 – Clap and touch

Aim   Ending game, to practise concentration.

What to do   See page 204.

CIRCLE MEETING 8

Remind the children of the circle rules (see page 202).

Activity 1 – Birthday game

Aim Warming-up game.

What to do See page 121.

Activity 2 – Faces 2

Aim To introduce the children to the theme of feelings.

What to do The children sit in an inward-facing circle. The teacher tells them she is going to 'put on' different faces. They are to try to guess what each face is (e.g., happy face, sad face, angry face, surprised face). The teacher tells the children that they can each have a turn at putting on different faces and instructs them which face to wear.

Open Forum

The teacher asks the children what people's faces tell us about them (i.e., how they are feeling). She asks the children if any of them is feeling unhappy about anything.

Activity 3 – Face pictures

Aim To develop awareness of body language.

What to do Collect magazine cut-outs of faces showing different emotions. Ask the children to say what they think each emotion is.

Activity 4 – Round: 'I feel happy ...'

Aim To end on a positive note.

What to do Using Talking Ted, each child completes the sentence: 'I feel happy when ...'. For example:

> 'I have some sweets.'
> 'I go to the seaside.'
> 'I play with my friends.'

CIRCLE MEETING 9

Remind the children of the circle rules (see page 202).

Activity 1 – Oranges and lemons

Aim   Warming-up game.

What to do   See page 104.

Activity 2 – Puppet show

Aim   To introduce the theme of feelings.

What to do   The teacher uses a glove puppet such as a rabbit who talks to the children. For example:

> 'Hello, children, I'm Ritzy Rabbit and this is my friend Talking Ted. You all know Talking Ted, don't you? I've got lots of friends in my school; can you guess some of their names? [Children respond.] I'm very sad today because Hiccup Hedgehog has been horrid to me. Can you guess what he did to me? [Children respond.] Can you help me? What can I do? How can I stop Hiccup Hedgehog saying nasty things to me? [Give time for response.] If children respond with ideas such as 'Hit him', 'Punch him', Rabbit replies, 'Oh, that won't work. It will just make him crosser. And anyway I know his big brother sometimes hits him and it doesn't help him to be a kinder person.'

When a child responds (and I promise you at least one will!), 'Talk to him', Rabbit asks the children what they would say to Hiccup Hedgehog. Rabbit endorses such suggestions as: 'tell him he's hurting your feelings', 'tell him he's being unkind', 'ask him to be nice to you', 'ask him to be your friend', 'ask him to play with you'. Ritzy Rabbit then thanks the children for all their help.

Open Forum

Ritzy Rabbit asks the children if any of them has had her feelings hurt by being called horrid names (the children must not name another child in a negative way; they should say 'someone'). Rabbit then asks the children to be very honest and put up their hands if they have called other children horrid names. Rabbit praises the children's honesty for owning up, and asks the children what they can do in the future (e.g., be kinder, don't hurt people's feelings, don't call anyone nasty names).

Activity 3 – Pass a smile

Aim   To end on a positive note.

What to do   See page 105.

Activity 4 – Choices

Aim   To reinforce their right to have their needs respected.

What to do   Hiccup Hedgehog and Ritzy Rabbit want to say 'Good-bye' to each of the children together by giving them a puppet kiss on each cheek at the same time but, as Ritzy says, 'You don't ever have to be kissed or touched if you don't want to. When we come round to each of you, please nod your head if you would like a kiss, or say "No" and shake your head if you don't want one and we'll wave our hands at you instead.' In this way each child's wishes are acknowledged and given attention as the teacher moves around inside the circle with her two puppets.

CIRCLE MEETING 10

Remind the children of the circle rules (see page 202).

Activity 1 – All change

Aim   Warming-up game.

What to do   See page 138.

Activity 2 – Puppet show

Aim To continue discussion of being kind.

What to do Ritzy Rabbit talks to the children. For example:

> 'Hello, children, do you remember me? What's my name?
> [Pause.] You really helped me last time and Hiccup Hedgehog
> has stopped calling me horrid names. I've got another
> problem this week, could you help me again? Some of the
> other animals won't let me join in their games. It makes me
> very sad.'

Open Forum

Rabbit asks if this has ever happened to any of them. How did it make them feel? Rabbit asks the children if they think it is fair of the other animals to exclude him. Why not? Comments will include: 'because it's mean', 'it's unkind', 'they're not being nice to you'. Rabbit asks what his animal friends and the children should do in the future. Answers should include: 'be kind', 'let other children join in', 'don't hurt anyone's feelings'. Rabbit thanks the children for their help and asks if they are going to be kinder and remember not to leave people out from their games.

Activity 3 – Teach me a game

Aim To help the children learn more playground games, to give playground games more status by bringing them into Circle Time.

What to do Ask the children to show the puppets what games they themselves know. They can demonstrate them in the middle of the circle.

Activity 4 – Ring o' roses

Aim Puppets and children share a fun activity together.

What to do The puppets pretend they don't know the words, so they hold 'hands' while the children sing them the words of the song. The puppets act out the words.

CIRCLE MEETING 11

Remind the children of the circle rules (see page 202).

Activity 1 – Musical islands

Aim   Warming-up game.

What to do   See page 148.

Activity 2 – Wizard Happy

Aim   To encourage kindness and thoughtfulness for others.

What to do   The teacher produces a special hat or cloak and tells the children that anyone who wears the cloak can be Wizard Happy and make a wish for something special for other people. The teacher puts on the cloak and makes a wish (e.g., 'I wish the sun would always shine at weekends and in school holidays.'). She tells the children that they can each have a turn at wearing the hat or cloak and making a wish for other people.

Open Forum

The teacher asks if any child is unhappy about anything that Wizard Happy might help them with.

Activity 3 – Round: 'I will be kind'

Aim   To consider ways of being kind.

What to do   The children think of a kind act that they will do that day for someone else and, using Talking Ted, each child completes the sentence: 'I will be kind and ...'. For example: 'let my sister play with my toys today', 'ask Tom to join in our football game', 'help Mummy put the tea things away'.

Activity 4 – Creative visualisation

Aim   To imagine being kind.

What to do   The teacher plays some gentle music. The children sit or lie with their eyes closed. The teacher asks them to imagine that they are playing happily in the playground when they see another child crying. They want to be kind and help the sad child. Ask them to imagine talking to her and think about what they would say. Imagine a reason why the child is crying. Think how they would help her. Think how they feel because they have been kind and helped someone.

CIRCLE MEETING 12

Remind the children of the circle rules (see page 202).

Activity 1 – Send a ripple

Aim   Warming-up game.

What to do   See page 132.

Activity 2 – Friends

Aim   To think about friendship.

What to do   The teacher shows the children a photograph of one of her own friends and tells them that it shows her friend. She asks the children why they think this person is a friend. Answers may include:

> 'because she's nice to you'
> 'because you like her'
> 'because you do things together'.

The teacher asks the children what they like about their friends, and what they do for their friends. She asks the children why it's important to have friends, and to think what it is like if you don't have a friend.

Open Forum

The teacher asks the children if any of them is sad because she does not have a friend at the moment. The teacher asks the other children how they could all help any children who do not have a friend (e.g., be nice to them, ask them to join in your games, be friendly, talk to them).

Activity 3 – Round: 'I like my special friend because ...'

Aim   To end on a positive note.

What to do   Each child in turn names a friend and gives one reason why she likes him or her. For example:

> 'I like my special friend because he's fun.'
> 'I like my special friend because she's kind.'

Activity 4 – Musical statues with mime

Aim   To have fun.

What to do   See page 129.

CIRCLE MEETING 13

Remind the children of the circle rules (see page 202).

Activity 1 – Birthday game

Aim   Warming-up game.

What to do   See page 121.

Activity 2 – Round: 'My favourite TV programme is ...'

Aim   To get everyone involved in talking to one another.

What to do   Using Talking Ted, each child in turn completes the sentence, 'My favourite TV programme is ...'.

Open Forum

The teacher asks the children what sort of make-believe games they enjoy playing. Why is make-believe fun? (Answer: because you can do anything you want.)

Activity 3 – Fantasy journey

Aim To practise make-believe.

What to do The teacher tells the children that she is going to take them on a make-believe journey with friends. They have to pretend all the things as she tells them. The journey can include: splashing in the sea, climbing a steep hill, crawling through exciting fields, making a snowman and so on.

Circle Meeting 13: Activity 3 – Fantasy journey

We are going to go on a journey now. I want you to imagine all the places that I tell you about and try to make believe that you are really there. You are travelling with all your friends and you are really looking forward to the journey. First of all you have to check your back-packs to see if you have everything you need: food, drinks, bedding, thick jumper, torch. When you're ready to start, put on your back-packs.

Right, off we go! [Teacher walks around with the children.] Look at the scenery. What can you see? Look, there are some cows in that field over there. What else can you see? On we walk. We reach a stile and have to climb over it. Now we're walking through a field. Mind your feet, don't step in any cow pats! On we walk, it's getting hotter and hotter. Can you feel the sun on your heads? Your packs seem heavier and heavier. You're sweating and thirsty. Oh, how hard it feels to walk. Slower and slower. Look, there's a stream over there, can we make it?

Here we are at the stream. Take off your shoes and feel the cool water on your feet. Take your back-packs off and find your nice refreshing drinks.

Time to go. Put on your shoes and your back-packs. We have to walk through a thick, dark wood now. Be careful of the branches and the brambles. Move them out of your way. See if anyone else needs help. It's so thick here we will have to crawl on our hands and knees very slowly and carefully. Mind that your hands don't get stung. Here we are at the end of the wood. We can stand up again now.

We have to climb a very steep mountain. It's hard work going up and up. Catch hold of a rock and slowly pull yourself up. Does anyone need a hand to pull her up? On we go, up higher and higher. It's beginning to get cold, we're so high. Let's stop and get our warm clothes out of our back-packs and put them on. That's better! Now we can go on. Can you see the top yet? Look, it's covered in snow. We're nearly there.

Feel the cold, cold snow. Shall we build some snowmen? Roll big balls for the bodies, now smaller ones for the heads. Look out for some stones to make the faces. Let's join hands and dance round the snowmen.

It's getting dark. We need our torches. Use your torches to see where you are going. Be careful as it's very dark. Take care where you tread and don't bump into anything. Look, there's the hut we're staying in. Let's go inside. It's time to get out your bedding and spread it on the ground. Lie down, close your eyes and think about all the things you've done on your journey.

CIRCLE MEETING 14

Remind children of the circle rules (see page 202).

Activity 1 – Animals

Aim To encourage imagination.

What to do The teacher tells the children that they are going to pretend to be different animals (e.g., lion, mouse, elephant, bear, horse etc.). The children mime being each animal as the teacher commands.

cat mouse   bear horse   chimpanzee

Activity 2 – Round: Pets

Aim To encourage the children to think on the spot and have confidence to speak aloud.

What to do The children take turns to tell the class about one of their pets. If a child does not have a pet she may talk about one she would like. Examples:

'My pet is a rabbit. He is called Snowy. He is white and furry. He likes to eat carrots. He can jump very high.'

'I would like a dog. I would call him Bingo. I would take him for walks and teach him tricks.'

Open Forum

The teacher asks if any child found it difficult to talk about her pet. Why was this? Answers may include: 'I get nervous talking', 'I couldn't think what to say.'

Activity 3 – Story cue

Aim   Fun, to encourage concentration.

What to do   The teacher tells the children a prepared animal story (see below). Each time she says certain cue words the children have to respond with a particular action, for example:

> lion – hands on heads
> elephant – tap knees twice
> monkey – tap shoulders twice
> tiger – stand up, turn round, sit down
> hippo – all move one seat to right.

Practise the actions several times before telling the story.

Circle Meeting 14: Activity 3 – Story cue

Lion and Elephant met in a jungle clearing. 'Oh, I'm very pleased to see you, Lion,' said Elephant. 'I need some help because I can't think of anything to give Hippo for his birthday.'

'It is a problem,' answered Lion. 'I can't think of anything either. Whatever shall we do?'

'Let's go and ask Tiger,' said Elephant, 'he's a clever chap, so he might have some ideas.'

Elephant and Lion set off together to look for Tiger. They found him lying in the sun, fast asleep on his favourite rock. 'Wake up, Tiger,' shouted Elephant. 'We need your help.'

The big stripey cat slowly opened his eyes and gave a yawn. 'Oh! Lion and Elephant,' he said sleepily. 'What is the matter with you?'

'Can you help us think of a birthday present for Hippo, please?' asked Lion. 'We just can't think of anything he'd like. All Hippo wants to do is lie in the water all day and squelch in the mud.'

'Oh dear,' answered Tiger. 'That's a hard thing to think about. I'm much too tired so, if you don't mind, I'll just go back to sleep again,' and he closed his eyes and began to snore.

Lion and Elephant looked at each other in dismay. 'Now what are we going to do about Hippo's present?' said Elephant.

Just then, they heard a rustle in the branches above them. Looking up, they saw Monkey, swinging from tree to tree. 'Hello, you two,' Monkey shouted down to them. 'Come and see what I've found.'

Lion and Elephant followed Monkey through the jungle, leaving Tiger asleep on his rock. Monkey stopped and pointed to a spiky object on the ground. It looked a bit like a prickly porcupine.

'Whatever is it?' asked Lion. 'I don't know,' Monkey answered. 'I've never seen one before.'

'I know what it is,' said Elephant. 'It's a people object called a broom, but the handle is missing. People use them to sweep their houses and paths.'

Lion looked at the broom for a minute and then began to smile. 'I've got a brilliant idea,' he said. 'We could give the broom to Hippo for his birthday present. He could use it as a scrubbing brush when he's lying in the river. He could scrub all the old mud off his body with it and then go and squelch in some nice, fresh mud.'

'What a good idea!' said Monkey.

'Even Tiger couldn't have thought of anything this clever,' said Elephant.

Elephant picked up the broom with his trunk. 'Come on, Monkey and Lion,' he shouted. 'Let's go and give Hippo this wonderful present.'

CIRCLE MEETING 15

Remind children of the circle rules (see page 202).

Activity 1 – Round: 'My favourite shop'

Aim   Warming-up exercise, to get everyone participating.

What to do   Each child in turn names her favourite shop and says why she likes it.

Activity 2 – Going shopping

Aim   To encourage speaking, memory.

What to do   The children are put into groups of 3. The teacher can include more able and less able children in each group. She tells the children they are going to play at shops. The groups are spread out around the room. If it is feasible the shopkeeper could stand behind a table. In their groups each child has a turn at being the shopkeeper and the other two are customers. The customers have to ask the shopkeeper for the items they want. The teacher can instruct the children to ask for two, three or more items according to the capability of the class. The shopkeeper mimes getting and packaging the items and giving them to the customer, repeating what the items were. The children mime paying, giving change and so on.

Open Forum

Did the children find the game easy? Did any child have any problems or find anything difficult?

Activity 3 – Send a ripple

Aim   Ending game.

What to do   See page 132.

CIRCLE MEETING 16

Remind the children of the circle rules (see page 202).

Activity 1 – Marching

Aim   Warming-up game.

What to do   See page 115.

Activity 2 – Round: 'My favourite sweet is …'

Aim To introduce the theme of sharing.

What to do Each child in turn completes the sentence, 'My favourite sweet is …'.

Development At the end of the round the teacher tells the children to imagine they each have a bag of their favourite sweets. They are going to mime offering the bag to other children, saying, 'Would you like one of my sweets?'

Open Forum

The teacher asks the children why it is good to share. Are there some things they have trouble sharing with others?

Activity 3 – Electric squeeze

Aim Ending game

What to do See page 129.

CIRCLE MEETING 17

Remind children of the circle rules (see page 202).

Activity 1 – Car, bus, lorry

Aim Fun, warming-up game.

What to do The children stand in an inward-facing circle. Each child in turn says 'car', 'bus' or 'lorry'. If any child gets the sequence wrong, she is out and sits down.

Activity 2 – Helping hands

Aim To introduce the theme of being helpful.

What to do The teacher tells the children she is going to open a door and mimes pushing the door. She says, 'Oh no, it's stuck. What can I do?' When a child suggests, 'Someone else should help,' the teacher asks the children if they will help. The teacher and children mime pushing. She says, 'The door is open now. Thank you for being helpful.'

The teacher mimes walking along, then stops suddenly and says, 'Oh no, there's a big tree trunk in my way.' She tries to lift it, saying, 'It's too heavy to lift.' She asks the children, 'Can you help me lift the tree trunk?' The teacher and children mime lifting. She says, 'Thank you for helping me lift the tree trunk.'

The teacher talks to an imaginary person, saying, 'Hello, Mr Balloon-seller. Yes, of course I'll hold your balloons.' She mimes taking balloons and says, 'Oh dear, there are so many I can't hold them all.' She asks the children, 'Will you each hold a balloon for me?' The teacher mimes giving each child a balloon to hold.

Open Forum

The teacher asks the children why it is good to be helpful to others. Does anyone need help with anything?

Activity 3 – Musical islands

Aim To reinforce the helping hand.

What to do See page 148.

CIRCLE MEETING 18

Remind children of the circle rules (see page 202).

Activity 1 – Clap and touch

Aim Warming-up exercise.

What to do See page 204.

Activity 2 – Being kind

Aim To encourage kindness.

What to do The children sit in an inward-facing circle. The teacher asks them to imagine that a child has fallen down in the playground and is hurt and upset. What should they do and say? The teacher encourages the children to express sympathy and show kindness. The children form groups of 3, one to play the hurt child and the other two to practise being kind and taking the appropriate actions. Children swap roles within their groups. Groups may also practise responding to other situations. For example:

> A child is upset because she has lost her new pencils.
> A child is upset because he has broken a toy brought to school to 'show' in class.
> A child is upset because she has left her reading book at home.

Open Forum

The teacher asks if any child is upset about anything and in need of sympathy.

Activity 3 – Send a ripple

Aim Ending game.

What to do See page 132.

CIRCLE MEETING 19

Remind children of the circle rules (see page 202).

Activity 1 – Oranges and lemons

Aim Warming-up game.

What to do See page 104.

Activity 2 – Sharing

Aim To encourage sharing.

What to do The teacher tells the class that they are going to pretend that they have a new toy. They are to imagine what the toy is and pretend to play with it. She tells them they must now find someone to swap toys with. They must tell the other child what their toy is and pretend to play with each other's toys.

Open Forum

The teacher asks the children if they mind sharing their toys at home with other children. What worries, dislikes and so on do they have about sharing their toys? Why is it good to share?

Activity 3 – Round: 'My favourite toy is ...'

Aim   Self-affirmation.

What to do   Using Talking Ted, each child completes the sentence, 'My favourite toy is ... because ...'.

Activity 4 – Duck, duck, goose

Aim   Fun.

What to do   See page 155.

CIRCLE MEETING 20

Remind children of the circle rules (see page 202).

Activity 1 – Simon says

Aim   Warming-up game.

What to do   See page 114.

Activity 2 – Drum beat

Aim   To encourage listening and concentrating.

What to do   The children sit in an inward-facing circle. The teacher places a drum and drumstick in the centre. She tells the children they must listen carefully because one of them will be chosen to repeat her drum beats. The teacher beats the drum (e.g., for four beats) and names a child who is to repeat this. This child repeats those beats, and then beats a different set of beats, naming another child to come and repeat the latest set. The game continues until all the children have had a turn. Encourage the children to try to vary the rhythm or volume of the beats.

Open Forum

The teacher asks the children what they liked or disliked about this activity.

Activity 3 – Marching

Aim Ending game, fun.

What to do See page 115.

FURTHER CLASSROOM ACTIVITIES

Affirmation Pages

Each child has a prepared worksheet on which to fill in personal details with the teacher's help. These are displayed on the wall.

Example

Name *Jane Rawlings*	
My favourite colour is	*Red*
My favourite activity at home is	*Playing with my Power Rangers*
My favourite food is	*Sausage and chips*
My favourite animal is	*A cat*
This is my shield	

Affirmation Tree

The teacher makes a card tree for display. Each child has a leaf on which she prints her name and something she is good at. The teacher can help the children prepare their statements.

Example

Balloon Chart

See page 109.

Achievement House

Each child is given a 'brick' on which to write her name and something she is good at. The teacher then displays the bricks as a 'house'.

Kind Flower Garden

Each child has a card flower. In the centre she writes one kind deed that she has done. She then colours the petals and leaves. The flowers are displayed as a garden.

Helpful Hands

The children draw around their hands, cut them out and write one helpful thing they have done on their hand. These can then be displayed.

Kind/Unkind Chart

The teacher displays a chart with two different coloured columns. The children ask for 'kind' or 'unkind' words to write in the appropriate column.

Example

Kind Words	Unkind Words
Share	Push
Care	Kick
Helpful	Unhelpful
Gentle	Nasty name-calling
Friendly	Bossy
Nice	Unfriendly
	Bad-tempered

Special Person Gallery

The teacher prepares card squares on which 'I am special' is written. The children bring in photographs of themselves to stick on their cards, which are displayed on the wall. The children decorate around their photographs, if they like.

Name: Sarah Marks

I am special

Family Tree

Children make up a tree of family members using photographs. Pets can be included. (See the warning about using this activity; page 109.)

Example

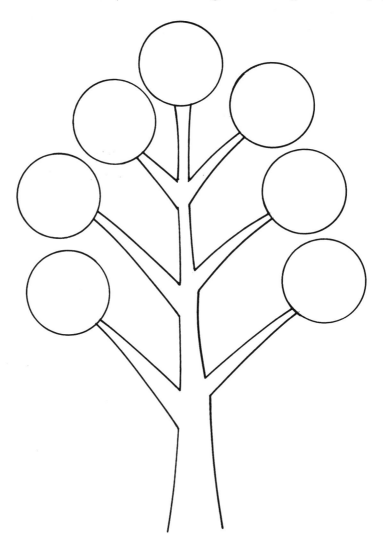

PARACHUTE GAMES

Parachute games provide an ideal opportunity for fun, co-operative games. It is best to spend some time with the children initially, learning how to work together to make ripples, mushrooms and so on. Children may take it in turns to be under the parachute, a few at a time, whilst the remainder make ripples and mushrooms above them. You will be able to buy a light circular piece of material called either a parachute or an activity canopy from some educational suppliers. Parachutes are available from the following:

Jenny Mosley Consultancies (Play Parachutes), 8 Westbourne Road, Trowbridge, Wiltshire, BA14 0AJ (01225 767157)

NES/Arnold (Education Division) (Spordas Parachutes), Ludlow Hill Road, West Bridgford, Nottingham, NG2 6HD (0115 945 2200).

It may also be possible to beg or borrow a real parachute from a local club.

Shout 'Hello'

The children stand around the parachute, holding it at waist height. On the count of 3, they raise their arms to make the parachute mushroom and shout 'Hello' to a player opposite.

Greetings

The children stand around the parachute, holding it at waist height. Two children, from opposite sides, are chosen to perform a greeting ritual; for example, shaking hands, 'give me 5.' On the count of 3, the children raise their arms to make the parachute mushroom. The two chosen players run underneath the parachute to the centre, perform their greeting ritual, then run back to their places. Two different players are then chosen and the game continues until all children have had a go.

Row the boat

The children sit cross-legged around the parachute, holding it with both hands. They all make gentle rowing movements and sing, 'Row, row, row the boat gently down the stream; merrily, merrily, merrily, merrily, life is but a dream.'

Making a tent

The children crouch down around the parachute, holding it with both hands. On the count of 3, they raise their arms to make the parachute mushroom, step forward under it, then pull it down behind them and sit on the edge of it. One child can stand in the centre to be the tent pole.

Storm at sea

A few children at a time lie on top of the parachute, in the centre. They are told they are on a small boat on the sea. The remaining children crouch or sit around the outside, holding the parachute in both hands. The teacher tells them to make gentle sea waves, then talks them through a storm, gradually increasing the wave movements at the same time. After the storm, the waves slowly decrease until the water is calm.

Change places

The children stand around the parachute, holding it at waist height. The teacher calls out a category (e.g., anyone with a birthday in December, anyone with a black dog, anyone with a 'G' in her name). Try to make the categories a bit exclusive, otherwise there will be no-one left to hold the parachute. On the count of 3, the children raise their arms to make the parachute mushroom. Any children in the named category have to swap places, running underneath the parachute. The game continues with different categories. (Try to ensure that every child is included in at least one category.)

Underground tunnels

The children sit or crouch around the parachute, which is on the ground. One or more players are chosen to name a player on the other side of the circle, then crawl under the parachute and tunnel in the direction of the child or children named. The other children ripple and shake the parachute, keeping it low, to try and disorientate the tunnellers. How many players manage to pop up exactly in the right place?

Deliver the parcel

The children stand around the parachute, holding it at waist height. An object such as a fairly light, smallish box is placed on top in the centre. The teacher names a child. All the children work together to ripple or tilt the parachute, so that the object on top is moved to the named player. This child then names another player and the parcel is moved on to that one.

Sunken treasure

A box containing treasure (any small items placed inside by the teacher) is placed in the centre under the parachute. The children stand around the parachute, holding it at waist height. When the parachute is mushroomed, children are chosen one or two at a time to go under the parachute, look in the box and retrieve a named item of treasure as quickly as possible.

When the children have had some fun and played a few games with the parachute, it is a good idea to hold a circle meeting and brainstorm their suggestions for variations or new parachute games.

> *I ordered a parachute and now my class earn time with the parachute for their good behaviour. All the infants stop to ask me when I am going to do some parachute work with them and it has been a great hit with the staff.*
>
> *(Teacher's comment)*

EXTRA CREATIVE VISUALISATIONS

1   We're going to close our eyes and imagine we're by the sea. The beach is miles of soft, white sand.

Think of the beach, it stretches as far as you can see. Imagine standing on the soft, warm sand. Feel your feet sinking into the softness. It feels so nice and comfortable.

Imagine that you are walking now, slowly. You lift one foot and place it down again, feeling it sink into the warm sand. Think of each step as you make it. Concentrate on the sand moving as you walk on it.

You look out to sea. It's the bluest blue you can imagine. You can see little glints of light where the sun reflects on the surface. Look at the water's edge, where the sea meets the sand. Gentle white waves break onto the shore. Imagine the sound of the waves. It's a gentle schlapp, schlapp noise. It makes you feel drowsy.

Think of lying down on the warm sand. Imagine your body sinking into comfort. Feel the warmth and softness under your arms, imagine burying your hands into the sand, then lifting them out and watching the sand grains trickle off.

You look into the blue sky. Small white clouds drift across. They look like cotton wool, they are so fluffy. You can see birds flying high up, swooping and gliding, graceful and quiet. You feel so peaceful and relaxed, it's such a nice place to be.

2   We're going to close our eyes and imagine a special secret place that belongs just to you. Each person is going to have his or her own place which is the safest place in the world.

Imagine what your safe place will be like. Perhaps it's by the sea, or in a cave, or a special room. Imagine looking round your own special place – does it have any furniture in it? If it does, look at the furniture closely. Imagine the shape of your furniture, think of the colours of each piece. Imagine touching each item, stroking it, patting it, feeling that it all belongs just to you.

What can you see around your own special, safe place? What is the scenery like? Everything about your place is comfortable and familiar.

What sounds can you hear – birds, singing, water? Anything else? The sounds are all nice, peaceful noises that you like to hear.

You love your safe place because you know that you can always go there whenever you are sad, angry or frightened and, because it is so perfect, you will soon feel better. Imagine how happy and contented you feel, being in your secret place with all your favourite things around you. You feel that it's the best place in the whole world.

3   We're going to close our eyes and imagine that we've been invited to the best feast in the world. Think about what you are going to wear. Imagine the details of all your clothes, the colours, shapes and materials. You are feeling really smart. You love the way you look.

Now it's time to travel to the feast. You can get there any way you wish – in a really super fantastic car, on a horse, in a horse-drawn carriage, in a space ship, on a magic carpet. Think of how you are going to travel to the feast. What does it feel like? What can you see on the journey? Imagine looking at your surroundings as you travel along.

You have reached your destination. Where is your feast being held – in a big marquee, in a palace, in a lovely wood or a meadow filled with flowers? Think of the place where your feast is. You are happy because it is such a nice place.

Now you can see all the tables of food and drink. What is on the tables? Imagine all the different things to eat. They are all your favourites.

Imagine reaching out and picking up something nice to eat. You pop it into your mouth. Think of the delicious taste of the food in your mouth. Imagine all the different things that you eat. Think of the taste of each one as you eat it. Now you feel full and happy.

This is the best party you've ever been to.

4   We're going to close our eyes and imagine we are under the sea on a coral reef. Think of the water, clear and blue, all around you. Imagine being buoyed up by the water floating, drifting gently along.

Hear the soft, rippling sound of the water around you. Look at the beautiful coral – pink, red, mauve, all sorts of fantastic shapes. You glide easily in and out of all the nooks and crannies. Look at the beautiful, bright fish – red, yellow, green, purple, black and white, striped and spotted. You have never seen such incredible fish before. Imagine them swimming around you. You can reach out and touch them. They feel smooth and silky. Watch them dart and dive and imagine yourself swimming with them, quick and skilful, turning smoothly through the water. You feel happy because you can swim so well and the fish are all your friends.

You see the wreck of a sunken ship and swim over to it. Imagine its broken masts and jutting edges. You swim inside and see a large trunk lying on the bottom. You swim up to the trunk and slowly, with great effort, lift up the lid.

The trunk is full of treasure. Imagine all the gold, silver, precious jewels. Pick up the treasure and look at it. It is so beautiful. Look at each item one by one. Look at the shimmering jewels, their bright colours sparkling. Look at the shining gold coins, bury your hands in them, hear them chink against one another.

You feel so happy in your wonderful, water world.

5 We're going to close our eyes and imagine that we are going on a journey to a magical land. A big silver spaceship has come to collect us. We are all sitting inside. It's ready to take off.

Imagine it has now started and is going faster and faster. Look out of your window and see the scenery whizzing by. Feel the speed of your spaceship, it's moving faster than you've ever been in your life before. Watch everything flashing by.

Now we have arrived at Rainbow Land. The spaceship stops and you walk off.

You look around you at the strange trees and flowers. Imagine trees with blue trunks and pink leaves, orange trunks and purple leaves, red trunks and yellow leaves. You are amazed at the bright colours.

You can see beautiful butterflies and birds. Imagine what they look like, all different colours. Small furry animals come to greet you. They are friendly and rub up against your legs. They too are brightly coloured, with spots and stripes. Imagine what they look like.

You bend down to stroke them, then pick them up and put your face on their soft, silky fur. It smells nice. You breathe in the sweet, pleasant smell and enjoy the feel of their warm furry bodies.

You look around at the houses. They are all brightly coloured as well. Notice all the different colours. Imagine a house that you would choose to live in. What is it like outside?

Imagine going into the house. What is the living room like? Think of the furniture you would have in it. Now think of the bedroom. Think of all the nice things you would have in the bedroom. Imagine lying on the soft, comfortable bed. You feel relaxed and happy because you are in such a wonderful land.

6   We're going to close our eyes and imagine that we are at a fairground. Think of all the rides you can see around you. Imagine all the sounds of the rides, people laughing, shouting, children squealing, stall owners calling for customers.

What can you smell? Hot dogs, burgers, candy floss, chips, sea food. Imagine all these noises and all these smells.

You are going on your favourite ride. Imagine yourself seated, excited and ready to go. The ride starts. You look around at the people and amusements flashing by.

Suddenly the ride zooms off up into the sky. You look down and see the people getting smaller and smaller. The ride goes on upwards, faster and faster. You can feel the wind rushing past your face.

You look down again. You can see whole towns and cities, rivers and mountains. Look at them all, they look like toy places.

On you travel, further and further. Now you see countries and the earth is no more than a big round globe. You look up and see the moon getting bigger and bigger.

Imagine all the rocks and craters on the moon. What do they look like?

Your ride circles round the moon and begins to travel back to earth. Imagine how it looks as you get nearer and nearer. You see countries, rivers, mountains, jungles, cities, towns, then people and the fairground. You can smell the fairground smells and hear the fairground noises again.

You are happy because this has been the most exciting ride of your life.

PART 5

Further Information

The Circle-Time model and the National Curriculum

Spiritual, moral and cultural development in the National Curriculum

Spiritual development is judged by how well the school promotes opportunities for pupils to reflect on aspects of their lives and the human condition. Circle-Time strategies provide regular weekly opportunities for children to discuss and consider the complexities of human nature and develop an awareness of spirituality and empathy for a range of human needs.

Moral development is judged by how well the school promotes an understanding of the moral principles which allow pupils to tell right from wrong and to respect other people, truth, justice and property. Circle Time fulfils these criteria through the formulation and practice of Golden Rules. Moreover, the games and activities, set out in themes with their clearly stated underlying moral values, allow the children to understand the benefits for both themselves and others of adopting good moral values and highlight the consequences and disadvantages of not following them.

Cultural development is judged by how well the school prepares to understand aspects of their own and other cultural environments. Again, the themed aspect of Circle Time raises cultural issues in a thoughtful and respectful way in order to promote understanding and tolerance of differing cultures.

Recommendation 5.2 is concerned with behaviour and discipline. Circle Time fulfils the evaluation criteria by promoting positive behaviour, individual and collective responsibility and self-discipline through its incentives and sanctions policies. These are effective because they aim to foster an awareness and appreciation of the greater benefits which intrinsic rewards bring to the individual. In other words, the system fosters a shift in discipline from teacher responsibility to individual child responsibility. It is able to achieve this because the caring and valuing ethos of Circle Time, the emphasis on peer encouragement and praise, the discussion and Open Forum phase all aim to raise the self-esteem of children. This, when combined with a programme of success through achievable targets of work and behaviour, allows a child to move away from negative behaviours to more fulfilling and positive ones. The move is complete when the child learns to exercise self-discipline.

English in the National Curriculum

Key Stage 1

1. Range
Pupils should be taught to listen carefully and to show their understanding of what they see and hear by making relevant comments. In considering what has been heard, pupils should be encouraged to remember specific points that interested them and to listen to others' reactions.

2. Key Skills
Pupils should be taught conventions of discussion and conversation, e.g. taking turns in speaking, and how to structure their talk in ways that are coherent and understandable.

Pupils should be encouraged to listen with growing attention and concentration, to respond appropriately and effectively to what they have heard, and to ask and answer questions that clarify their understanding and indicate thoughtfulness about the matter under discussion. They should use talk to develop their thinking and extend their ideas in the light of the discussion. They should be encouraged to relate their contributions in a discussion to what has gone before, taking different views into account.

How Circle Time fulfils these criteria

- Children are taught and practise the skills of thinking, looking, listening, speaking and concentrating.
- Rounds encourage all children to raise specific points and to listen to one another's responses.
- Discussion teaches children the skills of debate, i.e. thoughtful consideration and evaluation.
- Circle games require children to listen and respond to instructions.
- Circle games encourage children to share ideas and develop imagination.
- Circle activities give children the opportunity to practise sentence structure and expand their vocabulary.

Key Stage 2

1. Range

Pupils should be given opportunities to talk for a range of purposes, including:

> exploring, developing and explaining ideas;
> sharing ideas, insights and opinions.

Pupils should be given opportunities to participate in a wide range of drama activities, including improvisation, role-play, and the writing and performance of scripted drama. In responding to drama, they should be encouraged to evaluate their own and others' contributions.

2. Key Skills

They should be taught to listen to others, questioning them to clarify what they mean, and extending and following up the ideas. They should be encouraged to qualify or justify what they think after listening to other opinions or accounts, and deal politely with opposing points of view.

3. Standard English and Language Study

Pupils should be taught to use increasingly varied vocabulary. The range of pupils' vocabulary should be extended and enriched through activities that focus on words and their meanings, including:

> language used in drama, role-play and word games.

How Circle Time fulfils these criteria

- The Circle-Time model has a basic strategy that operates during Open Forum; that is, Plan, Do and Review.
- Children have an opportunity to identify any problem area. It could be concerning work, behaviour or a community problem. Then with the help of their peers they explore the range of options open to them and decide on an action plan which will be put into effect during the following weeks.
- This plan will be then brought back to a subsequent Circle Time, where the initiator and the class group will review its effectiveness.
- Circle Time includes a wide range of drama activities including puppets and improvisation, and a range of role play methods deliberately chosen to help the group explore any theme or current issue that concerns them.
- Warm-up exercises are often based on word games designed to encourage flexibility, memory and spontaneity. Through the circle the children are encouraged to address each other, to ask each other questions and to respond respectfully to differing points of view.
- A basic groundrule of Circle Time is that no child may make any negative personal comment to any other. This ensures respect at all times.

The school council as a quality circle

In an ideal world, it is good if a school can encourage the concept of school councils. A council could consist of two children from every class, plus one teacher representing the staff. They would agree to meet within the usual Circle-Time structure of groundrules. The role of the school council is to ensure that all children are consulted and listened to regarding any ideas or concerns relating to the school.

The following description by a Year-6 pupil gives an indication of how powerful an experience this can be.

School council

In the school council we discuss the problems of the school and how to make it a better place for everyone.

One of the things we discuss is football. Football was a problem because the boys did not let the girls play and if they did they made fun of them. The school council put a stop to this by not letting the boys do this any more. Anybody who did this was sent down to Mr Nolans. We have a school council every fortnight, Another problem we solved was children with packed lunches sitting with diners. Because they shared food. We warned the children not to do this any more and it worked.

Circles within circles
by Nick Peacey

The following description from Nick Peacey, Head of Special Educational Needs Joint Initiatives for Training at the University of London, was written after watching Circle Time take place.

Circles within circles: a lesson for us all?

The classroom is on the top floor of a Victorian primary school near King's Cross. It is hot and the noise from outside is distracting. Twenty-five 9-year-olds are sitting in a circle. They have been concentrating for over an hour. They are working under the supervision of a teacher they have never seen before.

And the discussion is moving into even deeper water. Tim puts up his hand in response to the question: 'Would anyone here like some help with behaviour?'

> 'I need some help because I keep getting mad and hitting people at lunchtime.'
>
> 'Is there anybody here who would like to help Tim?'
>
> Someone raised a hand. 'Yes, Sakira?'
>
> 'Would it help if you walked away from people when they start on you?'

'I have tried that already. They just keep following me, but
  thank you.'
'Yes, Delroy?'
'Tim, would it help if I stopped calling you names
  sometimes?'
'Yes, Delroy, that would help me a lot. Thank you.'

This is stirring stuff, all about feelings, and traditionally most un-British. This sort of discussion is hard enough with a group of adults. But these children are talking directly to one another about sensitive issues.

For this group feels safe. You can see it in the pupils' faces and body language. You can hear it in their responses in the discussion.

Confidence has been established through a series of carefully structured exercises. The pupils work to protect one another's self-esteem. In that way their own is preserved and enhanced.

They have learnt to signal when they want to speak. They have found out why failure is valuable: 'because we can learn from it'. They have learnt not to name individuals. 'I don't like it when someone pushes me in the dinner hall' produces more rational discussion than 'I don't like it when Melanie pushes me in the dinner hall.' The latter leads to 'I didn't push you', 'You did so' dialogues.

They have learnt the difference between laughing at someone ('pointy laughter') and with them. They have learnt the value of praise and something about how to accept it (even more un-British). They have learnt that they can collectively find solutions to problems.

Working in this sort of quality circle is usual enough in many industrial contexts (particularly in Japan). It is still unusual in schools though becoming established. It is, however, rarely used in school staffrooms, frequently the graveyards of teachers' self-esteem.

'I've been having some difficulties with 4M.'

'Really? They never gave me any trouble last year.'

On this afternoon, even more remarkably, the circle of hard-working pupils is surrounded by another circle – of adults. These observers are teachers receiving in-service training in the use of the Circle-Time approach. In the morning Jenny Mosley, the tutor, gave a theoretical and practical introduction (they worked in a circle) to the techniques. This afternoon they are seeing them in use, unrehearsed and with a class Jenny has never met before.

This is an important development in teacher training. Traditionally, courses on how to improve children's behaviour are for adults only.

They are frequently delivered in institutions far removed from the classroom. Now the work on behaviour has been opened up to view. All the messages that the normal course structure leaves unspoken and unseen are now available to all. Moreover, the process is taking place live, not in a 'made for television' format on a video display.

Both the adults and children gain a lot in a very short time. The class teacher, Juliet, says she's never seen her 9-year-olds work like this before. They are using every chance to help others in their class group (Jenny refers to them as a 'team'). The teachers have never attended a course like it. Their evaluations are unanimously enthusiastic: they want more days like this one.

We have all learnt our lessons today.

I, as in-service organiser for SENJIT, have learnt that enormous benefits can accrue if some teacher-training experiences are placed in the hands of the children working with a skilled teacher.

The children have learnt that they hold the key to creating the climate in which good learning and positive relationships can flourish.

The teachers have learnt that they don't need to be the only ones to try and sort out things that go wrong – they can consult and then work with the children to find the solutions.

Jenny Mosley's Circle-Time approach is not a new-fangled, trendy innovation. It has been tried and tested, for years in many schools. It works, most importantly, because it is grounded in a sound psychology. This solid foundation in theory means that the methods do not break down after being used in school for a short time, and that they can be used with anyone. Barnsley, Belfast and King's Cross kids have all benefited recently from Jenny's input.

Circle-Time methods can also be used with adults, whether on a course or in a school. Jenny Mosley, when working in a school with concerns about children's behaviour and self-esteem, will begin with Circle Time for the staff. This has to be on an equal opportunities basis. Caretakers and lunchtime supervisors will be included as all too often poor relationships in classrooms can be exacerbated by poor relationships among staff. High self-esteem and the resulting energy it releases among staff are the keys which unlock successful learning experiences for the pupils. *This is a lesson the government needs to attend regularly.*

Resources

Back up training and support for Jenny Mosley's Circle Time Model

Training manual

Mosley, J. (1993) *Turn Your School Round*, LDA (from LDA, Duke Street, Wisbech, Cambridgeshire, PE13 2AE). A Circle-Time approach to the development of self-esteem and positive behaviour in the primary classroom, staffroom, and playground.

Training courses

Key people may be trained either to go back to their school or their LEA as certificated trainers responsible for supporting all adults and children in their community through the *Turn Your School Round* model.

Jenny Mosley's Turn Your School Round Consultancies offers Saturday workshops, summer schools and booklets for any person wishing to learn more about the approach.

Becoming a Circle-Time consultant

Should you wish to train in this approach in order to become a freelance consultant with the Turn Your School Round company, training programmes and summer schools are available. Ask for further details and an application form from Jenny Mosley, Turn Your School Round Consultancies (see over).

Training support for your workplace

Turn Your School Round Consultancies has highly qualified personnel trained in the various areas of the Circle-Time model available to visit your workplace to give courses and workshops to all your teaching and support staff.

INSET courses

The following courses are available from Turn Your School Round Consultancies:

Turn Your School Round – an introduction

A whole-school approach to building self-esteem through Circle Time

Assessing the effectiveness of your self-esteem, anti-bullying and positive behaviour policies

Raising morale through team-building

Practical activities to maintain the power of Circle Time

Equal opportunities

Curriculum enrichment

Drama and creative arts

Play therapy: an introductory course.

Send a large stamped addressed envelope to:

Turn Your School Round Consultancies
Collingwood
8 Westbourne Road
Trowbridge
Wiltshire
BA14 0AJ

Further qualifications in this approach

University of Bristol

Jenny Mosley runs 3-day modules for a specialist MEd in Guidance and Counselling (BPS recognised). Information is available from Jacqui Upcott, University of Bristol, School of Education, 35 Berkeley Square, Bristol, BS8 1JA; telephone 01179 287046.

The modules are:

> Developing positive relationships
> Counselling in groupwork
> Creative arts in therapy and education.

University of London

Jenny runs a series of single Circle Time/Turn Your School Round awareness raising days for SENJIT.

She also runs a 10-day course in Quality Circle Time as part of an Advanced Diploma award.

For information contact Nick Peacey, Co-ordinator: SENJIT, University of London Institute of Education, 20 Bedford Way, London, WC1H 0AL; telephone 0171 612 6305.

Joining the Circle-Time network

If you do not wish to undertake any further training, but would like to have news about how far these ideas are developing and about the latest approaches, initiatives and any forthcoming conferences, you may become a member of the Turn Your School Round Network, which intends to have its own newsletter and regular seminars.

Self-Esteem Network

The Self-Esteem Network is an educational charity set up to promote self-esteem in policy and practice. Details are available from Titus Alexander, 32 Carisbrooke Road, London, E17 7EF.

Useful organisations

Young Minds

22a Boston Place, London, NW1 6ER; telephone 0171 724 7262.

Forum for the Advancement of Educational Therapy and Therapeutic Teaching

Idonea Taube, Membership Secretary, 50 Marquis Road, London, NW1 4HP.

Association of Playtherapists

Lynn Bennett, Bucklands Cottage, Cholsey, Wallingford, Oxfordshire, OX10 9HB.

Books

Books to help you with your own self-esteem

Mosley, J. and Gillibrand, E. (1995) *She Who Dares Wins*, London: HarperCollins.
Steinem, G. (1993) *Revolution from Within: A Book of Self Esteem*, Corgi Books.
Turner, C. (1994) *Born to Succeed*, Element.

Books to inspire you

Axline, V.M. (1964) *Dibs: In Search of Self*, Penguin Books.
Cheifetz, D. (1971) *Theatre in my Head*, Boston: Little Brown & Co.
Harrison, B. (1986) *Sarah's Letters: A Case of Shyness*, London: Bedford Way Papers.
Holt, J. (1969) *How Children Fail*, Pelican Books.
MacCracken, Mary (1974) *Circle of Children*, Philadelphia.
Oaklander, V. (1978) *Windows to Our Children*, Moab, UT: Real People Press.
Winnicott, D.W. (1980) *The Piggle*, Penguin Books.

Books on theoretical background or research on, or relating to, self-esteem

Benson, Jarlath F. (1987) *Working More Creatively with Groups*, Tavistock Publications Ltd.

Burns, P. (1979) *The Self Concept*, London: Longman.

Burns, P. (1982) *Self Concept Development and Education*, Rinehart & Winston.

Glasser, W. (1965) *Reality Therapy*, NY: Harper & Row.

Glasser, W. (1967) *Schools without Failure*, NY: Harper & Row.

Greenhalgh, P. (1994) *Emotional Growth and Learning*, Routledge.

Lawrence, D. (1987) *Enhancing Self Esteem in the Classroom*, Paul Chapman Publishing.

Mead, G.H. (1934) *Mind, Self and Society*, Chicago: University of Chicago.

Rogers, C.R. (1961) *On Becoming a Person*, Boston: Houghton Mifflin.

Rogers, C.R. (1980) *A Way of Being*, Boston: Houghton Mifflin.

See also the Reference section at the end of the first chapter in Part Three: Some theoretical underpinnings of Circle Time.

Books with further useful practical ideas for self-esteem building

Borba, M. and C., *Self-Esteem: A Classroom Affair*, Vols. 1 & 2, London: Harper & Row.

Brigman, G. and Earley, B. (1990) *Peer Helping: A Training Guide*, Portland, ME: J. Weston Walch.

Capacchione, L. (1982) *The Creative Journal for Children: A Guide for Parents, Teachers and Counsellors*, Shamhala Publications Inc., Massachusetts 02115.

Cattanach, A. (1992) *Playtherapy with Abused Children*, London: Jessica Kingsley.

Dewar, R., Paslet, K. and Notley, M. (1989) *Games, Games, Games*, London: The Woodcraft Folk.

Dixon, D. (1990) *Teaching Young Children to Care: 37 Activities for Developing Concern for Others*, Twenty-Third Publications, Mystic, CT 06355.

Dixon, D. (1990) *Teaching Young Children to Care: 37 Activities for Developing Self-Esteem*, Twenty-Third Publications, Mystic, CT 06355.

Feest, G. (1992) *Listening Skills: Activities for Primary School Children and Their Teachers*, Southgate Publishers Ltd.

Forth, G. Hans and Wactus, H. (1974) *Piaget's Theory in Practice – Thinking Goes to School*, Oxford: Oxford University Press.

Fugitt, E.D. (1983) *'He Hit Me Back First!'*, Jalmar Press, California 90274.

Hertfordshire Education Services (1994) *The Child as a Citizen*, Hertfordshire Education Services.

Home Office, *'You, Me, Us!'*, Crack Crime, PO Box 999, Sudbury, Suffolk, CO10 6FS.

Illsley-Clarke, J., *Self-Esteem, a Family Affair*, London: Harper & Row.

Jacobs, M., Turk, B. and Horn, E. (1988) *Building a Positive Self-Concept: 113 Activities for Adolescents*, Portland, ME: J. Weston Walch.

Jennings, S. (1993) *Playtherapy with Children*, Oxford: Blackwell Scientific Publications.

Kingston Friends Workshop Group (1985) *The Handbook of Kingston Friends Workshop Group, Ways and Means: An Approach to Problem Solving*.

Masheder, M. (1986) *Let's Co-operate*, Peace Education Project.

Masheder, M. (1989) *Let's Play Together*, Green Print, The Merlin Press.

Mosley, J. (1989) *All Round Success*, Wiltshire County Council (available from Advisory Education Services, County Hall, Trowbridge, Wiltshire, BA14 8JB).

National Primary Centre, *Practice to Share 2: The Management of Children's Behavioural Needs*, Birmingham: National Primary Centre.

Prutzman, P., *The Friendly Classroom for a Small Planet*, CCRC.

Schrank, J. (1972) *Teaching Human Beings: 101 Subversive Activities for the Classroom*, Boston: Beacon Press.

Stoate, G. (1984) *Dramastarters*, Surrey: Thomas Nelson and Sons Ltd.

Thacker, J., Stoate, P. and Feest, G. (1992) *Group Work Skills: Using Group Work in the Primary Classroom*, Southgate Publishers Ltd.

Wetton, N. and Cansell, P. (1993) *Feeling Good; Raising Self Esteem in the Primary Classroom*, Forbes Publications.

White, M. (1992) *Self Esteem – Its Meaning and Value in Schools: How to Help Children Learn Readily and Behave Well*, Daniels Publishing.

Some recent books on Circle Time/Self-esteem

Bliss, T. and Robinson, G. (1995) *Developing Circle Time*, Lame Duck Publications.

Bliss, T. and Tetley, J. (1995) *Circle Time*, NASEN Enterprises Ltd.

Curry, M. and Broomfield, C. (1994) *Personal and Social Education for Primary Schools through Circle Time*, NASEN Enterprises Ltd.

Fitzpatrick, P., Clarke, K. and Higgins, P. (1994) *Self-Esteem*, The Chalkface Project.

Books giving lots of ideas for happier lunchtimes and playground games

Ashley, B., *Dinner Ladies Don't Count*, Young Puffin.

Blatchford, P. (1989) *Playtime in the Primary School (Problems and Improvements)*, NFER-Nelson.

Dalbeattie Primary School, *Yesterday's Games Tomorrow*, video and booklet pack, Bright Sparks, Dalbeattie Primary School Enterprises, Dalbeattie, Dumfries and Galloway.

Deshpande, C., *Five Stones and Knuckle Bones*, A. & C. Black.

Happy Heart Playgroup Pack (1992) Thomas Nelson.

Learning through Landscapes, 3rd Floor, Technology House, Victoria Road, Winchester.

Masheder, M., *An Educational Pack – Let's Co-operate*.

Mosley, J., *Guideline for Midday Supervisory Assistants in Primary Schools*, Wiltshire Education Advisory Services, Courtney Hall, Trowbridge, Wiltshire.

Mosley, J. (1993) *Turn Your School Round*, Cambridge: LDA.

National Playing Fields Association, *Great Playtimes Games Kit*, London: National Playing Fields Association.

National Primary Centre, *The Management of Children's Behavioural Needs* (pack: *Practise to Share*, video: *395 to Lunch*), National Primary Centre, Westminster College, Oxford.

Opie, P. and I. (1969) *Children's Games in the Street and Playground*, Oxford: Oxford University Press.

OPTIS (1987) *Lunchtime Supervision – The OPTIS GUIDE*, OPTIS House, Cricket Road, Cowley, Oxford.

Orlick, T. (1979) *The Co-operative Sports and Games Book (Challenge without Competition)*, Writers and Readers Publishing Co-op.

Pax Christi (1980) *Winners All – Co-operative Games for All Ages*, Pax Christi, St Francis of Assisi Centre.

'Playgrounds in the Primary School', *Teaching Today*, BSS, PO Box 7, London.

Ross, C. and Ryan, A. (1990) *'Can I Stay in Today, Miss?' Improving the School Playground*, Trentham Books.

Singing Games for Children, TELSTAR Video, London.

Wilmer, D. and Chamberlain, M., *The Playground – Story Book for 4–6 Year Olds*, Collins.

Books and organisations to recommend to help parents

Hartley-Brewer, E. (1994) *Positive Parenting: Raising Children with Self Esteem*, Mandarin Paperbacks.

Gingerbread, 35 Wellington Street, London, WC2 7BN; telephone: 0171 240 0953.

National Council for One-Parent Families, 255 Kentish Town Road, London, NW5; telephone 0171 267 1361.

Parent Network, 44–6 Caversham Road, London, NW5 2DS; telephone: 0171 485 8535.

Relate (marriage guidance), Herbert Gray College, Little Church Street, Rugby, CV21 3AP; telephone 01788 573241.

Stepfamily, 72 Willesden Lane, London, NW6 7TA; telephone: 0171 372 0844.

Related reading

Axline, V.M. (1969) *Play Therapy*, Penguin Books.

British Association of Counselling (1995) *Counselling and Psychotherapy Resources Directory 1995*, British Association of Counselling, 1 Regents Place, Rugby, Warwickshire, CV21 2PJ.

Clive, T. and Baldwin, S. (1994) *Selective Mutism in Children*, London: Whurr Publishers.

Hanko, G. (1985) *Special Needs in Ordinary Classrooms*, Oxford: Basil Blackwell.

Mosley, J. (1994) *You Choose*, Cambridge, LDA; a handbook for staff who work with *adults* with learning difficulties, to help promote self-esteem and self-advocacy.

I have endeavoured to include as many useful resources as I can. Nevertheless the gaps in my knowledge are huge and the space in this book is diminishing, so I have to leave out many valuable books and organisations which I hope to include in the next edition.